HOW TO ANALYZE PEOPLE

PEOPLE

Body Language and Behavioral Psychology. The Definitive Guide to Reading People Fast and Accurately (2022 Guide for Beginners)

Sienna Griffith

CONTENTS

INTRODUCTION

All reading requires concentration, even if only for a moment. Speed reading, however, re ure utaned, forceful concentration because when you peed read, you do many thing at once. To peed read well, you mut een and read the word on the page, reman alert to the author' man ideas, think along with the author. You have to know when to km, when to read fat, and when to low down to get the get of the get of the get of the get of

This book contains proven tips and strategies for reading and analyzing people's nonverbal geture and body language. The nformation here wil help you undertand how tudy another' body language, decpher different peronalty type and how the goal of reading is to comprehend what you read. How well you understand what you read is determined by your reading speed, vocabulary size, and degree of familiarity with the subject matter.

When done correctly, analyzing people is a very valuable skill. A lot can be revealed about a person based on how they speak, act, and even do things unconsciously. Very analyse based a lot on the envronment that you're analyzng them n. To have sucess n life, you have to understand the concept and keep workng on t.

Understanding other people's behavior may be one of the most underappreciated abilities for a human being. If that sounded a better exaggerated to you, convence yourelf and make a change NOW!

Even as we communicate with one another, we must pay attention to small details such as gestures and sights, because communication isn't just about words. Actually, communication is a rather complex process that makes our entire being speak what's in our hearts and minds.

Reading other people's body language is a skill that we develop throughout our lives. It's a automatic process in which we calculate other people's inner thoughts based on their nonverbal movements. That's without even realizing we're doing it. Though it works both ways, others judge us in the same way.

If something shakes your confidence, demonstrate some understanding. Don't berate yourself. Learn from what happened, consider what you could have done differently, and remember it for the next time. Talk about what happened with someone who cares. Then, remind yourself of your strengths and the things you've accomplished.

Get back into the game!

CHAPTER 1
How Can Anyone Read People?

How To Read People

Being perceptive about other people's feelings and thoughts is an important skill that will help you navigate interpersonal relationships. Even though each human is unique, we are all, on some level, wired the same. Here's how to get targeted wth recognzng even the mot fleeting of ubtle cue.

1.   Establishing A Baseline

1. Recognize the eron: To be able to read someone, you must first know them well. By gettng to know omeone personally, you'll have a better deal of what ther lke or dlke are, what ther common habt are, and what Bae your opnon of other on every encounter wth them, not jut on 1.

People may act and speak differently depending on the situation. For example, you may have a frend who I very fdgety. If so, their fdgetting may not be a in of lyng or nervoune. If you meet them on the treet, common knowledge would deem them nervou or anxou. Nope. They simply have an exciting leg.

Pay attention to the habtory of others. Do they keep an eye on you all the time? Do they change theIR voce when they're nervou? When they're preoccuped, how do they tranmt themselves? The will key you nto what you hould be lookng for when trying to read them.

2. k pen-nded ueton: When you read something, you are watching and listening. What you're not doing is grabbing the conversation by the horn and tearing it in your drecton. So get your ueton and get outter there. Stay back, relax, and enjoy how.

1. OPEN-ENDED QUESTIONS well allow them to talk more o you can oberve them longer.

2. You'll bet off akng to-the-pont, pertinent ueton. If you ask, "How's your family?" you might get a rambling, all-over-the-place response that doesn't help you gauge well the information you're lookng for. If you ask, "What book are you reading readly?" You might be able to gather more personal information.

3. Search for ncontence n theIR Baelne: normally affectonate peron who seems not to be phycally preent and doen't eem to want to get near anyon wth a 10-foot pole Once you've gathered how the peron act n day-to-day life, keep an eye out for that doen't meh.

1. If something doesn't seem to add up, you'll have to ask why, at the very least. They may be exhauted, fought with their gnfcant other, got yelled at by their bo, or jut have ome mall peronal ue that' Do not assume it is a reflection of your relationship with that person before you have all of the details.

4. Work and luter: Seeng one cue not good for jumpng to a concluon. After all, one may be leanng away from you merely becaue char is hard to get comfortable n. If you are heavily relying on the non-verbal, make sure you have three or four in before you begin adding.

1. Try to get a cue from ther word, ther tone, ther body, and ther face. It may be afe to proceed once you get one from each and they all lneup. But, of course, a good way to accertan if you're correct jut to be drect and ak.

5. Recognize Your Weaknee: As a mortal human, you are prone to fallibility. Just like the Pope. When you see something nice, chances are you'll like it. If you're wearing a fnely-talored fnely-talored fnely-talored fnely-talored fnely

You're probably going to truth an Italan suit. Should you? Not snecessarily.

1. Dangerou people generally thnk of dangerou people a drunkard roamng the treet unbathed and carryng a knfe. Most psychopaths are charming and have their act together. Though take control of, be aware that your subconscious tells you to judge a book by the cover when that' necessarly the best or most accurate

2. Paying Attention To Boday Language

1. Observe how they are holding themselves: Body language can tell you a lot about how someone is feeling, especially how comfortable they are. It may be a reflection of the topc at hand, or it may be one new new new new new new new new new new new new new new new There are some general guidelines that ndcate comfort level.

Negative r Uncomfortable Body Language cue:
- Leanng away from you
- Crossed arm or leg
- Lookng away when talking
- Lmb that are movng a lot of nervou tap of the fnger or leg

2. Examine Their Face: You should also keep an eye out for fleeting facial expressions. Watch people very cloely to earn if any mall movement of the mouth get away what people are feelng. For example, a peron may mele at you, but if they twtche, that may mean that they are thinking of omethng negatve.

1. nyther clenched or tene, even for a econ, can be a gn. a furrowed brow, a tene jaw, t'all in of anxety

2. If they cloe for longer than a normal blank, they're probably tallng and taking a monent to get a grap on a tuaton. It generally an ndcator of someone who is long grap, be t on themselve or in a tuaton

3. Check to see if they touch you. For example, if a peron uually hugge you when they see you but don't, that may mean that they feel tenon toward you. Think about things like a weak handhake — that could gnfy nervoune or uncertanty.

1. Touch a tough one, though. Everybody has a different idea of a "personal bubble," and just because someone touches you a lot doesn't needly mean you're "n." You could jut be one n a line around the block. If you're worried about their tutoring habits toward you, watch them around other people to see where the norm is.

4. Examine how far away they are patal. How close or far away a person is from you also gives you some insight into their mental state. For example, if a peron dancing themelve from you physically, they may mean they do not want to be vulnerable or ntmate. Or it could mean they're in a hurry! Clusters are key here, gan.

1. Some people are not comfortable beng when a certan phycal proximity of other regardle of the tutory. So just because someone keeps their distance, it may not be a reflection of you. The ame goe for the antern end of the pectrum other people have no concept of peronal pace. If they're volatng your, they may not really really really really really really really really really really really really really re

5. Think about it. The Relevance of ULTURaL Relevance f Their BODy Language: People's cultural backgrounds will influence the language they use in their bodies, their facial expressions, and how close they are to you. It's critical to keep these things in mind when trying to read people. You don't want to draw the wrong conclusion about someone just because you saw them through a narrow len.

3. regte Vocal Cue 1. Lten To TheIR TONE OF VOICE: A person's voice can tell you a lot about how they're feeling. Leten for tone inconsistencies ptch of theIR voce are they coming off a happy and anger? They're probably trying to cover something up.

Noting the volume, are they talkng louder or ueter
Wait to see if they are hedgng ung their voce, saying "Um," or "Uh," often. If the cae, they may be nervou or lying and tryng to buy tme.

Check to see if their tone conveys an emotion that they aren't expressing. For example, do they look arcatc or angry? They may feel the need to pavely addre the situation. If the cae, it' better to get everythng out n the open. One major pychologcal According to research, 7 per cent of our communication comes from words, 38 per cent from the tone of voice, and 55 per cent from body language.

2. Write down the length and tone of their response: Short, clpped repone to ueton could mean that the person frutrated or buy, where long repone could mean that the peron ntereted and

3. Consider Word hoce: When people say something, there'alway a proce underlyng the content. If someone were to say to you, "You're dating another dental hygiene?" Their uage of the word "another" ndcate that they're ayng, "You jut dated a dental hygienist and that went to crap — now you're

1. The recent construct "yeah, no" has become quite popular. Even a mall two-letter word can be a dead giveaway for ambvalence (or for defntene or face-avent or aent or dent Even if your buddy says, "Dude, c'mon," that can be a mall in. The "dude" there to ndcate solidary, an acceptable way of ayng "frend." So get parng away those words to get a true ndcator of how your target feel.

4. READING PEOPLE IN DIFFERENT CONTEXT

1. Know The Proproprate Tell n Romantc ontext: On a date, you want to enure that the other peron alo love you. gan, clusters are u It is very common for people (women especially) to be mtaken a ntereted when they're jut beng sociable. So be alert.

What are is they leaning for body language? Do they have relaxed body language (no croed arm or tene houlder)? These are good guns that the peron feels comfortable and ntereted in you. On a date, try to ee how more the other peron talkng and how engaged, they are n the converation. If they are interested, they will lean forward, nod when you talk, and ak ueton.

Look at how much they're smiling. If they are tene and are not smiling during the entre date, they may feel uncomfortable. See how they approach you at the end of the date. This is when you should be especially aware of the interaction. Do they recognize you or hug you? Or do they remain far away? This will give you some insight into how they feel about you.

2. Know The ontruct f Job ntervew: Job ntervew can be nerve-wrackng and t can be difficult to gauge how well one went. Keep an eye out for positive body language that indicates that the interview is going well. But know that n the context, both parte are on HGH alert for good mpreon, o the data pont you gather may not be accurate

Again, make ure that the ntervewer give potve body language language language language language language language language langua You want them to show that they're interested in you and what you're saying. If your ntervewer is huffing paper or checking her or her computer creen or phone, they may be long nteret. Try to reclaim their attention if they appear to be bored or distracted. When you leave, observe how the ntervewer bids you farewell. Do they give you a firm handhake and a genuine mle? These are good in that mean the ntervew went well.

3. Detect Lar: One of the most common reasons why you would want to learn how to read someone is to see if they are lying. When observing someone see if they are lying, you want to look for body look for body look for body look for body look for body look for body look

Language and cue correlated with nervoune Once more: cluter.

Check to see if someone's voice has changed, or if they have changed their body language. For example, if your poue uually hug you a lot but uddenly top when you're akng them about omethng, they may be lyng. Do not mtake a peron who look to the de or doesdon't make eye contact for a lar becaue reearcher have found no relation between

Check to see if they stop using the word "I." Investigate how that ometme when people want to distance themselves. themelve from a le, they will avode ung the word "I" and will ntead peak of themelve n third peron (example: "Th guy love a good football

Check to see if what they're saying is too elaborate and detailed. When people le, they rehear an entire tory beforehand. If this is the case, keep an eye out for a story that has been rehearsed or overplayed.

They fidget and move around a lot. That a dead gveaway that omeone nervou. If the peron you're talkng to keep movng around, tappng ther foot, or chewng on a pencil, they may be lyng. Look nto ther eye, if ther pupl grow better when ayng omething, then t a le, that' why most poker players wear unglae.

When telepathy sounded like a uperpower, readng omeone' mind can be learned. From anticipating a student's needs to understanding how to approach your boss, developing a nner ntuton about what other value can help you get ahead.

"Perceptve people are alway more ucceful n life and work," "Top performer aren't alway the martet people; they're the one

People gnal about their thoughts all the time, Mner, but it can take practce to tune n. "When the meage you receve ay that the perondon't on the ame page, there are clue that are tellng you tep back and redrect," he said. "It's ti me to change the converation or your approach." There are five ways to read someone's mind—or, at the very least, take an educated guess—and build a better business relationship:

1. **Begin with General DIFFerences**

Understanding someone's generation can give insight into how he or she thinks. It's a len through which they see life.

"General diference are fascinating," "Mllennal often hde behand computer and peak ther mend through Twttr and blog." They do not place value on face-to-face communication. On the other hand, boomer like to talk to omeone n person."

Understanding someone's generation will help you know the better way to approach them to develop a relation. "If we're clong a deal wth a mllennal, we know there're no need to fly out and chedule a roundtable."

Different things have different values in generaton. For example, Mllennal look for fat result. "When we talk to them, we talk about uccome, proven procee," he ay. "Boomer are more conervatve. When we talk to them, we move lower and talk about things like safety and risk."

2. Recognize the Hot Buttons

another way to tell what omeone thnk to look for their pan pont, whch entails akng the right ueton. It is critical to establish a personal bond to learn what they consider to be important. "What a tragger emotion for them?" "Where are they comfort zone?" he ak "You must have large ears and a small mouth."

I recommend kppng pre-canned converaton and entering the relatonhp a decuon. "k open-ended ueton that allows the person to hare their trength and challenge," "Or tore about what you've done for other." One out of ten people will agree that they have the same problem, which will help you better understand what they require."

3. **Think about Personalities**

It can help to notice and oberve ndvual qualities to determne who they are as a peron and what' more more more more more more

He's very analytical, and he relates well when people lay out their ideas methodically: "I've taught my team that they have to come to be prepared to back up their ntat "If you don't, you've lost me."

Look for clues into someone's personality by paying attention to characteristics and verbage. Someone who prefers to be domnant, for example, may have an overly from handhake, says Mner. People who are welcome humor wilt often nsert arcam nto a converation. Use these clues to determine their value and approach.

4. Seek Nonverbal Communication

Nonverbal behaviour is also important, and Mner suggests watching for body language clues. If someone leans n, they are engaged. If they back up, look down, or turn away, they aren't listening to what you're saying. The tone of voice can also provide clues. For example, if one is anwerng you n monotone, they are mot likely unattached to your concept and not ntereted. When they look at you when you speak and move closer, they're fINDING value n what you're ayng.

5. Be a Good Listener Finally, lten to what omeone ayng and what they're not ayng. While this harder when the converationationationationationationationat Mner ay an engaged or paonate voce obvoutly on done over the phone. It's also apparent when omeone frutrated "Their tone must change, or you will hear a sigh," It is critical to developing a good ear that can lten for the ubtle ound. Anything critical or involving emotion should never be communicated via email, as it can be a real hindrance to being respectful."

CHAPTER 2
Body Language

Body language is a type of nonverbal communication. Body language about uer communcation behavor. This form of communcation I ued by both people and anmal. A portion of the behaviour is done ubconcouly. It differs therefore from communicating ung sign language, for example. Communication in sign language is intentional, but communication in body language is not.

What Exactly Is Body Language?
Body language the process of communcatng noverbally through body movement and geture. Positive body language can be defined as nonverbal movements and gestures that communicate interest, enthusiasm, and a positive reaction to what others are saying. How you

communcate wth your body I mportant becaue reearch how that 60% to 90% of communication I nonverbal. To many, body language is the most important aspect of communication because it expresses how we truly feel. You can learn how to nterpret the body language of thoe around you whle perfectng your own wth the class on the secrets

In general, body language controlled by our ubconcou mind and not alway followng what we ayen. The perceptive individual will be able to pick up on the differences between what you are saying with your words and what your body is saying with its movements and deduce how you feel to make certain you are

Practice your body language so that your movement matches your words when conveying your thoughts and opinions about how you want.

Body posture, gestures, facial expressions, and eye movements are examples of behaviour used in body language. Body language may provide clues as to a person's attitude or state of mind. It may ndcate aggreon, attentiveness, boredom, a relaxed state, pleasure, amuement, and ntoxcation.

Body language is important for communication and relationships. It relevent to management and leadership in bune and also in places where many people can be oberved. It can also be relevant outside of the workplace. It is frequently useful in datng, matng, family ettng, and parentng. Although body language I non-verbal or non-poken, it can reveal more about your feeling and meanng to other and how other reveal their Body language gnal happen on a concou and unconcou level.

The Body Language Vocabulary
Body language is less exact than spoken language, so you must be careful how you present it. certan movement or facal expression may be very meanngful, or may mean nothing. As a starting point, the following section will provide you with some common body language terms and their generally-accepted meanings.

Body Language POSITIVE

Positive body language I generally relable and cator of a peron' feeling. It gnal nterest the other peron and the conversation.

1.Poture Relaxed: Comfortably seated relaxed breathng, no visible stiffness or abrupt movement These ndcate no major barrer to commucation.

2.Relaxed arm and hand open (palm up or otherwise veble to the other person) are gn of openne.

3.Good eye ontact: Looking in the other peron' eye, especially when they are peaching, indicates nterest n that person. Proper eye contact nvolve lookng away occaonally to avolve start.

4.Nodding greement: When nods are used to punctuate important things said by another person, they gnal agreement, nteret, and undertanding. However, continuous unconscious bobbing of the head uually ndcate that the listener tuning out.

5.Take Note: Show nteret and nvolvement, especially if note are on what the other peron is ayng.

6.Smiling/adding Humor: This is a very positive sign. It gnal a warm personal relationship.

7.Leanng Cloer: Reducing the distance between two people, especially when one of them is speaking. Indcate nteret is up, and barrer is down.

8.Geturng Warmly: Talkng wth hand, especially wth palm open, ndcate invervement in the converaton and openne to the other person.

9.fantate Movements: You can how empathy wth mere agreement actions lke noddng your head or smiling.

10.Taking Notes: Taking notes lets others know that you value what they are saying and that you are involved in the conversation. Taking note is not appropriate in every situation

11.Slower: Take a deep breath, hold it for a second or two, and then exhale. Focus on slowing down your breathing and body movements. This will make you appear more confident and persuasive.

It will also help you relax if you are nervous. Moderation I the rule for all of these positive geture. When they are exaggerated, they can become more negative than positive. These actions inform people that you are on their side and that you can help them.

Identify wth their plght You can even utlize laughter when approprate.

Body Language NegatIVE

Negatve body language is less reliable as an indicator of a person's comfort with the current situation than positive body language. negative actions may jut be a matter of comfort for the peron, may ndcate that the peron I tred, or may reult from other matter

1.Body Tene: Stffne, wrnkled brow, jerky body moton, hands clasped n front or palms down on the table These can indicate a concern with the topic or deal wth the other person.

2.rm Folded n Front: Creates a barrer; can expre retance to what been added.

3.Hand on the Face: hand over one' mouth is a cloed geture. Boredom can be communicated by leaning on one's elbow with the can in the hand.

4.Movng around a lot, playng with the thing, and drumming fnger are usually a in of boredom, nervoune, or mpatence.

5.rms BehIND The Head, Leanng Back: The can be a relaxed geture in a well-etablhed relatonhp. It often ued to expre a dere for control or power in a new relatonhp.

6.Yawning: Boredom, perplexity. The other person is talking too much or in too much technical detail.

7.Impatience: Attempting to nterrupt what the other person saying, opening one's mouth fre uently as if to peak.

8.Dtracton: yeer flckng around, blank stares, flppng through literature wthout really readng it, lookng at others n the office, lookng at the

9.Leaning away: trongly negatve vodng moving cloer, even when omethng handed to the person.

1O. Negative Facial Expreon: These nclude shaking head, narrowed eyes, scowling, and frowning.

Varieties of Verbal Communication
Verbal communication includes ound, word, language, and peech. Speaking is an effective way of communicating and expressing our emotions in words. This mode of communication is further classified into four types, which are as follows:

1. Communcation interperonal
This mode of communication is extremely private and restricted to ourselves. It includes the lent conversations we have wth ourelve, wheren we juggle role between the ender and recever who are processng our thought and When a communication process is analyzed, it can either be conveyed verbally to someone or remain a thought.

2. Interpersonal Communication
The form of communication takes place between two individuals, resulting in a one-on-one conversation. Here, the two individuals nvolved wilt swap the roles of ender and recever to communcate more openly.

3. Communcation of Small-Group
This type of communication can take place only when more than two people are involved. The number of people will be mall enough to allow each participant to nteract and convert wth the rest. Press conferences, board meetings, and team meetings are examples of group communication. Unless a specific issue is being debated, small

group discussions can become chaotic and difficult to nterpret by everybody. This lag in understanding information completely can result n mcommuncation.

4. Communcation PUBLIC

This type of communication occurs when one individual addresses a large group of people. lecton campanges and publc peeche are examples of the type of communcation. In such cases, there is uually a single ender of nformation and everal receivers who are being addreed.

Nonverbal connection

Learn how to read and ue body language to build better relatonhp at home and work.

What Exactly Is Body Language?

While the key to success in both personal and professional relationships lies in your ability to communicate effectively, it is your nonverbal cues or "body language" that speak the loudest. Body language the ue of phycal behavor, expressions, and mannerm to communcate nonverbally, often done unconsciously rather than consciously.

Whether you're aware of it or not, when you interact with others, you're constantly giving and receiving wordle gnal. All of your nonverbal behavor, the geture you make, your poture, your tone of voice, and how many eye contact you make send strong They can put people at ease, build trust, and draw others to you, or they can offend, deceive, and misunderstand what you're trying to convey. These messages do not stop when you stop speaking. Even when you're lent, you're still communicating nonverbally.

In some cases, what comes out of your mouth and what you communicate through your body language may be two different things. If you say one thing but your body language says something else, your lener will most likely think you're lying. For example, if you say "yes" while shaking your head no. When confronted with such mingled gnal, the letener must decide whether to believe your verbal or nonverbal meage. Because body language is a natural, unconscious language that conveys your true feelings and intentions, they will most likely choose the nonverbal message.

However, by improving how you understand and use nonverbal communication, you can express what you mean, connect better with others, and build stronger, more rewarding relationships.

Why Does Nonverbal Immunotherapy Matter?

The way you lten, look, move, and react tells the person you're communicating with whether or not you care, if you're being truthful, and how well you're listening. When your nonverbal signals match the word you're saying, it increases trust, clarity, and response. When they don't, they can generate tenon, trust, and confuon. If you want to be a better communicator, you must become more sensitive not only to the body language and nonverbal cues of others but also to your own.

Nonverbal ommuncation and FIVE Role:

1. It repeats and often strengthens the meage you're makng verbally.

2. Contradiction: It can contradict the message you're attempting to convey, implying to your listener that you may not be telling the truth.

3. It can be used as a substitute for a verbal message. For example, your facial expression may convey a far more vvd meage than words can ever.

4. Completion: It may add to or complement your verbal meage. a bo, if you put an employee on the back in addition to giving praise, it can ncrease the employee's meage's meage's meage's meage's meage's meage's meage's meage'

5. It may accent or underline a verbal meage. Pounding the table, for example, can underline the message's message's message's message's message's message's message's

Nonverbal communcation TYPE

Many different types of nonverbal communication or body language include:

1.Face xpreon: The human face extremely expreve, able to convey countle emoton wthout ayng a word. facal expressions are universal, unlike other form of nonverbal communcation. The facal expreon for happne, adne, anger, urpre, fear, and dgut are the ame acro culture.

2.Body Movement and Poture: Consider how the way people t, walk, tand, or hold their head affects your perception of them. The way you move and carry yourself communicates a wealth of information to the rest of the world. Nonverbal communication includes your posture, bearing, tance, and the smallest movements you make.

3.GetureS: GetureS are woven nto the fabrc of our day lve. You may wave, point, beckon, or ue your hand when arguing or speaking anmatedly, often expressing yourself with geture wthout thinking. However, the meanng of some geture can be very different acros culture. When the OK in made with the hand, for example, convey a potve meage in english-speaking countre, to condered offensive n countre uch a Germany, R So, to avoid misinterpretation, be careful about how you ue geture.

4.eye contact: Since the visual sense is domnant for most people, eye contact is especially more more more more more more more m The way you look at someone can communicate a variety of emotions, including nteret, affection, hostility, or attracton. Ye contact also mantantant the flow of conversation and for gaugng the other peron' nteret and repone.

5.Touch: Through touch, we communcate a great deal. Consider the very diferent meage given by a weak handhake, a warm bear hug, a patronizing pat on the head, or a controlling grip on the arm.

6.Space: Have you ever felt uncomfortable dure a converation becaue the other person wa tandng too clook and invading your pace? We all re ure physical pace, though that need differentiation.

Depending on the culture, the situation, and the cloene of the relatonhp You can use physical space to communicate many different nonverbal messages, such as gnal of ntmacy and affecton, aggression, or domnance.

It's not just what you say, but also how you say it. When you speak, other people "read" your voice in addition to listening to your words. They pay attention to your timing and pacing, how loud you speak, your tone and nflecton, and sounds that convey understanding, such as "ahh" and "uh-huh."

How to Improve Nonverbal Communication

Nonverbal communication is a fast-moving back-and-forth process that necessitates your full attention on the moment-to-moment experience. If you're planning what you're going to do next, checking your phone, or thinking about something else, you're almost certain to make a nonverbal cue and not fully comprehend what's being communicated. You can manage tre and develop your emotional awarene by learning to manage tre and develop your emotional awarene.

Learn To Manage Stress In The Moment

Strive to demonstrate your ability to communicate. When you're stressed out, you're more likely to misunderstand other people, send confusing or off-putting nonverbal gnal, and fall into unhealthy knee-jerk patterns of behaviour. and remember: emotions are dangerou. If you are upset, you are very likely to make another upset, making a bad situation worse. Take teme out if you're feeling overwhelmed by tre. Take a moment to calm down before you jump back into the conversation. Once you've regained your emotional e q uilibrium, you'll feel better e q uipped to deal with the situation in a positive way.

The fastest and surest way to calm yourself and manage stress at the moment is to employ your senses what you see, hear, smell, taste, and touch or through a soothing movement. By viewing a photo of your child or pet, smelling a favorite scent, listening to a certain piece of music, or s q ueezing a stress ball, for example, you can quickly relax and re-focus. Since everyone responds differently, you may need to experiment to find the sensory experience that works best for you.

Develop Your Emotional Awareness

To send accurate nonverbal cues, you need to be aware of your emotions and how they influence you. You also need to be able to recognize the emotions of others and the true feelings behind the cues they are sending. This is where emotional awareness comes in.

Being Emotionally Aware Enables You To:

- Accurately read other people, including the emotions they're feeling and the unspoken messages they're sending.
- Create trust in relationships by sending nonverbal signals that match up with your words.
- Respond in ways that show others that you understand and care.

Many of us are disconnected from our emotions especially strong emotions such as anger, sadness, fear because we've been taught to try to shut off our feelings. But while you can deny or numb your feelings, you can't eliminate them. They're still there and they're still affecting your behavior. By developing your emotional awareness and connecting with even the unpleasant emotions, though, you'll gain greater control over how you think and act. To start developing your emotional awareness, practice the mindfulness meditation.

How To Read Body Language

Once you've developed your abilities to manage stress and recognize emotions, you'll start to become better at reading the nonverbal signals sent by others. It's also important to:

1. **Pay Attention To Inconsistencies**: Nonverbal communication should reinforce what is being said. Is the person saying one thing, but their body language conveying something else? For example, are they telling you "yes" while shaking their head no?

2. **Look At Nonverbal Communication Signals As A Group**: Don't read too much into a single gesture or nonverbal cue. Consider all of the nonverbal signals you are receiving, from eye contact to tone of voice and body language. Taken together, are their nonverbal cues consistent or inconsistent with what their words are saying?

3. **Trust Your Instincts**: Don't dismiss your gut feelings. If you get the sense that someone isn't being honest or that something isn't adding up, you may be picking up on a mismatch between verbal and nonverbal cues.

Evaluating Nonverbal Signals

1. **Eye Contact**: Is the person making eye contact? If so, is it overly intense or just right?

2. **Facial Expression:** What is their face showing? Is it masklike and unexpressive, or emotionally present and filled with interest?

3. **The Tone Of Voice**: Does the person's voice project warmth, confidence, and interest, or is it strained and blocked?

4. **Posture And Gesture:** Is their body relaxed or stiff and immobile? Are their shoulders tense and raised, or relaxed?

5. **Touch**: Is there any physical contact? Is it appropriate for the situation? Does it make you feel uncomfortable?

6. **Intensity**: Does the person seem flat, cool, and disinterested, or over-the-top and melodramatic?

7. **Timing And Place**: Is there an easy flow of information back and forth? Do nonverbal responses come too quickly or too slowly?

8. **Sounds**: Do you hear sounds that indicate interest, caring or concern from the person?

Understanding Body Language And Facial Expressions

Body language refers to the nonverbal signals that we use to communicate. According to experts, these nonverbal signals make up a huge part of daily communication. From our facial expressions to our body movements, the things we don't say can still convey volumes of information.

- It has been suggested that body language may account for between 60 percent to 65 percent of all communication.
- Understanding body language is important, but it is also essential to pay attention to other cues such as context. In many cases, you should look at signals as a group rather than focusing on a single action.

Here's What To Look For When You're Trying To Interpret Body Language.

Facial Expressions
Body Language - Facial Expressions
Think for a moment about how much a person can convey with just a facial expression. A smile can indicate approval or happiness. A frown can signal disapproval or unhappiness. In some cases, our facial expressions may reveal our true feelings about a particular situation. While you say that you are feeling fine, the look on your face may tell people otherwise. Just a few examples of emotions that can be expressed via facial expressions include:

- Happiness
- Sadness
- Anger
- Surprise
- Disgust
- Fear
- Confusion
- Excitement
- Desire
- Contempt

The expression on a person's face can even help determine if we trust or believe what the individual is saying. One study found that the most trustworthy facial expression involved a slight raise of the eyebrows and a slight smile. This expression, the reearcher suggested, convey both frendlne and confdence.

Facial expression is also one of the most unusual forms of body language. The expreon ued to convey fear, anger, adness, and happiness are malar all around the world. Research even suggests that we make judgments about people's intelligence based on their face and expression. One study discovered that ndvdual with narrower faces and more promnent noe were more likely to be perceived a intelligent. People wth long, joyful expreon were also judged as more intelligent than those wth angry expressions.

The eye
EYe - Body Language

The eyes are fre uently referred to a the "windows to the soul" nce they are capable of revealing a great deal about what a peron You engage in converation with another peron, taken number of eye movements a natural and mportant part of the communication proce. Some common things you may notice include whether people are making direct eye contact or averting their gaze, how much they are blinking, or if their pupils are dilated. When evaluating body language, attach to the followng eye gnal:

1. **eye Gaze:** When a peron looks directly nto your eye when havng a conversation, they ndcate that they are interested n and paying attent Prolonged eye contact, on the other hand, can be frightening. On the other hand, breaking eye contact and frequently looking away may ndcate that the peron I distrated, uncomfortable, or trying to conceal her real feelng.

2. **Banking:** Banking is natural, but you should pay attention to whether a person is blinking too much or too little. When people are stressed or uncomfortable, they tend to blink more quickly. Infrequent blinking may indicate that a person is attempting to control his or her eye movement. For example, a poker player may blink le frequently becaute he purpoely tryng to appear unexcited about the hand he wall deal

3. **Pupl Sze**: Pupl ze can be a very nonverbal communcation signal. While light levels in the environment control pupil dlaton, some emotions can also cause minor changes in pupil ze. For example, you may have heard the phrase "bedroom eye" used to decreate the look omeone get when they are attracted A hghly dlated eye, for example, can ndcate that a peron I interested or even arounded.

THE MOUTH
Mouth Language - Body Language

Mouth expreon and movement can alo be eental in readng body language. For example, chewng on the bottom lp may ndcate that the ndvdual experience feeling of worry, fear, or necurity. Covering the mouth may be an effort to be polte for the peron yawning or coughng, but it may alo be an attempt to cover up a frown of Smlng may be one of the best body language gnal, but mle can also be nterpreted n many ways. mle may be genuine, or t may be ued to expre fale happiness, arcam, or even cynicism.When evaluatng body language, pay attent to

1. Pured Lp: Tightening the lp may be an ndcator of date, dapproval, or dtrut.
2. People ometme bite their lp when they are worried, anxouted, or stressed.
3. Covering The Mouth: When people want to hide an emotional reaction, they may cover their mouth to avoid displaying mle or mrk.

4.Turned Up r Down: Slight changes in the mouth can alo be ubtle indicators of what a person feel. When the mouth is slightly turned up, it may indicate that the person is happy or optimistic. On the other hand, a slightly down-turned mouth can be an indicator of adne, dapproval, or even an outrght grimace.

Gestures
Geture - Body Language
Geture can be one of the most detailed and obvout body language signals. Waving, pointing, and using the fingers to ndcate numercal amounts are all very common and eay to undertand geture. Some geture may be cultural, however, givng a thumb-up or a peace gn in another country may have a completely different meaning than it does The following examples are jut a few common geture and their possible meanings:

Clenched ft can indicate ager n one situation or solidary n other.

Thumbs up and thumbs down are frequently used as geture of approval and disapproval.

The "okay" gesture, made by touchng the thumb and ndex finger n a crcle while extendng the other three fnger, can be ued to mean "okay" the symbol a vulgar geture I a vulgar geture I a vulgar geture I a vulgar geture I a vulgar geture I a vulgar geture I a vulg

The V gn, created by liftng the index and middle finger and eparatng them to create a V-hape, means peace or vctory n one country. When the back of the hand is facing outward in the Unted Kngdom and utrala, the symbol takes on an offenve meaning.

The rmnd Leg Body Language - rm

The arm and legs can also be ueful nonverbal nformation nformation nformation nformation nformation nformation nformat Crong the arm can indicate defenvene. Crong legs away from another person may ndcate dlke or dcomfort with that ndvdual. Other subtle gnal attempt to seem larger or more commanding when keepng the arms cloe to the body may be an effort to When evaluating body language, pay attention to some of the following signs that the arms and legs may convey:

Croed arm may indicate that a peron feel defensive, elf-protective, or cloed-off.

Standing with hand placed on the hp can be an indication that a peron I ready and n control, or t can be a gn of aggressiveness.

Clasping the hand behind the back may ndcate that a peron feelng bored, anxious, or even agry.

Rapidly tapping fingers or fidgeting can be a sign that a peron ha bored, mpatent, or frutrated.

Croed leg can indicate that a person is feeling cloed off or need of privacy.

Posture

How we hold our bodies can also serve as an important part of body language. The term posture refers to how we hold our bodies as well as the overall physical form of an individual. Poture can convey a wealth of nformation about how a peron feelng a wealth of nformation about peronalty characteristics, such as whether Sitting up straight, for example, may indicate that a person is focused and paying attention to what is going on. On the other hand, sitting with the body hunched forward can imply that the person is bored or ndfferent.

When attempting to read body language, try to notice some of the gnal that a peron' poture can end.

OPEN POSTURe entails keeping the trunk of the body open and exposed. The type of posture ndcate frendlne, openness, and wllngne.

Closed posture entails holding the trunk of the body, frequently by hunching forward and keeping the arms and leg croed. This type of poture can be an ndcator of hotlty, unfrendline, and anxety. Have you ever heard one refer to their need for peronal space? Have you ever felt uneasy when someone stands just a little too close to you?

The term proxemc was coined by anthropologist dward T. Hall, refers to the dance between people and the they nteract. Just a body movement and facal expreon can communcate a great deal of nonverbal nformaton, o can this phycal space between individuals.

Hall Decrbed Four Levels Of Socal Dtance That Occur n Different Situations:
1. **Intimate Distance 6-18 nche**: The level of phycal distance often indicates a closer relatonhp or greater comfort between ndvdual. It uccurres mostly during ntmate contact uccurred uccurred uccurred uccurred uccurred uccurred uccurred uccurred uccurred uccurred uc
2. **Peronal Dtance 1.5 TO 4 Feet**: Physical dtance at the level uccurrently between famly members or cloe freends. The closer the people can stand while interacting can be andcator of the level of intimacy in their relatonhp.
3. **Social Dtance 4 To 12 Feet**: This level of phycal detance I uantance uantance uantance uantance uantance uantance uantance uantance uantan With one you know fairly well, uch

as a co-worker you see several times a week, you may feel more comfortable interacting at In cases where you do not know the other person well, uch a potal delivery drverIf you only see her once a month, a distance of 10 to 12 feet may be more comfortable

4. **Publc Dtance 12 To 25 Feet**: Phycal dtance at this level is often ued n publc peakng tuaton. Speaking in front of a class full of students or giving a presentation at work are both good examples of such situations.

It is also important to note that the level of personal detance that ndvdual need to feel comfortable can vary from culture to culture. One oft-cited example is the difference between people from Latin culture and those from North America. People from Latn countries tend to feel more comfortable tandng closer to one another as they interact, whereas those from North merica need more person

Difference Between Verbal and Nonverbal Communication
verbal communcation the ue of audtory language to exchange nformation wth other people It may include sounds, words, or speaking. The tone, volume, and pitch of one's voice can all contribute to effective verbal communication.

Non-verbal communication is communication between people using nonverbal or visual cues. This includes gestures, facial expressions, body movement, timing, touch, and anything else that communicates without speaking.

When it comes to verbal communication, the other anwer does a good job. So I'll concentrate on nonverbal communication.

Nonverbal communication is communication between people using nonverbal or visual cues. The nclude body language (knec), the distance between people (proxemc), voice ualty (paralanguage), and touch (haptc). Based on these considerations, nonverbal communication communicates just as much, if not more, than verbal communication.

For example, if a peron has an angreve facial expression, enter nto an aggreve stance (knec), encroache upon another peron'

vew, even if the verbal communication sounds neutral. Nonverbal cues trump all verbal cues.

Another consideration is that even in written text, there is nonverbal communication such as handwriting style, padding, and the like.

In conclusion, communication is both verbal and nonverbal, demonstrating that human communication is more complex than it appears.

Views, Negotation, and Reflection

Body language can alo help you stay calm n situations where emoton have the potent to run high, for example, a negotaton, or a performance Use the following tip to defuse tension and demonstrate openne:

5. **1.Use Mirroring**: If possible, subtly mirror the person you're speaking to's body language. This will make him feel more at ease and allow him to build resilience. But don't copy every geture that he make, a th wll lkely make he feel uncomfortable, or that you're not takeng he
6. **2.Relax our Body**: It can be difficult to keep emotion at bay, especially nerve-wrackng situation lke an nerve-wrackng situation However, you can maintain the appearance of calm by keeping your hand still and avoiding fidgeting with your hair or touching your face.
7. **Look ntereted**: as suggested above, touchng your face or mouth can signal dhonety. However, it can also demonstrate that you are thinking.

CHAPTER 3
Understanding Self

Self and Identity are a subfield of psychology. As the name implies, it deals with issues of self-esteem and decency. The major area of nvetgation are elf-concept, elf-eteem, and elf-control. Self and Identity ncorporate element from variou area of pychology. However, it owes a particularly large debt to personal and social psychology. What dtnguhe elf and dentty a dcpline t centfc character. mpha based on empirical testing of ytematic theore about relevant phenomena. As a result, t methodology l approach varies from phloophy to sociology.

Individual Level Analysis Of the Self

There are variety of analyze that one can utlize to look at self and dentty. For example, one level of analy the elf on the ndvdual level elf-tate, elf-motve, elf-esteem, elf-efficacy, et cetera. Self-tate are elf-proceeds that include unbaed elf-awarenenene. However, self-motives are more erou mpule to act, onether than an nate and societal or cultural analy of the elf. The other level of analy I on the social or cultural level, for example, the cultural concepton of a peron, cultural arrangement that ma

Self-teem Collectve

Attude to ocal group ha an effect on the individual's elf-eteem toward their group and other group. The collectve elf-eteem gathered from each group depend on how they are treated. If the ndvdual ha low self-esteem, the outlook on other group can be negative, and bonding with other group can be difficult to manage in the future. The way mnorty group treat each other ha the kind of effect within the group, while treatng other groups ha the kind of effect within the group experence working with that group. Regardless of the group diference, some ndvduals who have a positive perceptve of another mnorty group can increase the ndvdual's collectve elf-eteem,

Cro-group

frendhholdholdholdholdholdholdholdholdholdholdholdholdholdhol dholdholdholdholdholdholdholdholdholdholdholdh " As a result, we hypothesized that high-quality cross-group friendship would foster a sense of collective self-esteem among majority group members. In turn, collectve elf-eteem I likely to fed collectve action tendence "'.

When the nner group ha potvty, HGH- ualty relaton, and reSPECT, they can ncreae collectve elf-eteem and collectvty within the communty. The psychological well-being of those who share a cross-racial friendship will increase. Different elf-seems are ued dependently on the diferent relaton hared wth the ndvual. The relational self refers to the aspects of the self-concept that are rooted in interpersonal attachments and shared with a significant other (e.g., family, friends). The collective elf refers to an aspect of the elf derived from membership in a social group (e.g., ethnic group). These relatonhip harded from one person to the next can be described as one's elf and dentity. The self-esteem described in the preceding paragraphs may vary depending on the individual's outlook on life.

The family and freed can be a contributing factor to each person's HGH or low self-esteem een. Socal dentity can be related to collective elf-eteem becaue both relate to how an individual contributes to the group to which they belong. Being able to UNDERSTAND the role that one take within their group, whether that group be ethnc, local cla, or any other group, the individual doe wha Having a connection to another group can contribute to some change, which may be positive or negative depending on the ndvdual's collective elf-eteem.

Recognize Yourelf
Before a woman sits on a rock and begins searching for a potential caregiver, it is beneficial to spend time understanding herself, including her capabilities, experience, and personal worth. Being self-aware can help you plan development and make career decon that are really for you. It's critical to understand what you want from your career, what will bring you fulfilment, and the type of environment or work culture in which you will thrive. This can help you target the type of professional development opportunity that will benefit you the most.

Develop Your Talent
- Consider the magnificent points of achievement or challenge in your life to date.
- Why are they magnificent?
- What have you learned from them, and how might they influence the type of career path you pursue?

Recognize Your Personalty Type
Understanding your personality type can often prove the key to recognize why you have a tendence to act or react a certain way and help de.

Understand Your Value and Motvation
What are your value and motivation?
How far do they form the foundation of what you conder career SUCCESS? What ele

Audt Your apablity and Expertise

- What do you consider to be your area of expertise?
- What knowledge and ualte do you have as a result of your research, pad or voluntary work experience, or hobby?
- What capabilities or competencies are present, and how can you bridge the gap?

Understanding our Learning Style

Identifying the mot effectve method of learning can nform the type of training or development you could take to develope.

CHAPTER 4
Behavior Analysis

Behaviour analysis is rooted in the behaviourist tradition and makes use of prncple learning to educate about behaviour change. While some branches of psychology strive to comprehend underlying cognition, behavioural psychology is unconcerned with the mental causes of behaviour and instead focuses on the behaviour itself. Behavor analy have robut practical application n mental health treatment and organzatonal pychology, especially when foc Behavior analysis is frequently used to develop abilities in children and adults with disabilities, to increase academic skills in school, and to enhance employee performance.

What I Behavior naturally?
The behaviour I analy a natural cence that eek to undertand the behavor of ndvdual. That behavor analyt, tudy how bologcal, pharmacologcal, and experental factor factor factor factor factor factor factor Recognizing that behaviour is something that individuals do, behaviour analysts place a special emphasis on studying factors that relatively influence the behaviour of individuals, an emphasis that that that that that that that that that that that that that that that that that that that tha The centure of behaver analysis has made discoveries that

have proven ueful in addressing ocally mortal behaver, such as drug taking, healthy e

What do you do naturally?

Behavior nally a centfic tudy of the princple of learning and behaver. The field of cence is concerned with describing, comprehending, regulating, and changing behaviour. They seek an answer by examining biological and environmental factors.

Although they are predominantly interested in the envronment's role in behavor change.

To the feld, there are three man branches: Conceptual Behavior naly, xpermental Behavior naly, and ppled Behavior naly The Conceptual branch focuses on the philosophical, theoretic, historical, and methodological issues that underpin the field. Experimental Behaviour natually nvolve bac reearch wanted to add knowledge about phenomena that control and nfluence behavior to the bod pplied Behavor natually focued on the applICAtion of the princple of behavor to the need of ndvual to promote behavor. make a difference and improve the ualty of life.

Expermental nd ppled Behaviour nally

There are two major areas of behaviour analysis: experiential and applied.

- EXpermental behavor analy entails bac reearch degned to add knowledge about behavor to the body.
- On the other hand, pled behavor analy focued on applying the behavor princple to real-world textual textual textual text

Those who work in the field of applied behaviour are intrinsically interested in behaviour and its relationship with the environment. Rather than focusing on nexternal state, B therapt focuses on obervable behaviour and employs behavioural techniques to bring about behavioural change.

ACCORDING TO THE Behavor nalyt CERTIFICATION Board:

"Professionals in applied behaviour analysis engage in the precise and consistent application of principles of learning, including operant and reflective learning, to address behavioural needs. XampleS of the applaction nclude: building the kell and achevement of chldren n chool ettemplete; enhancing the development, a"

Techn ue and Strategy

Several technology ues ued by behavor analysts include:

1. **Channg**: The behavor technology ue entails breaking a task down into smaller components. The simplest or initial step in the procedure was taught first. After that take ha been learned, the next take can be learned. TH CONTINUES UNTIL THE END e uence uccuply chaned together.
1. **Prompting**: This approach entails the use of some type of prompt to elicit the desired response. This may involve using a verbal cue, such as telling the person what to do, or a visual cue, such as displaying a picture designed to cue the response.
4. **Shaping**: The trategy entails gradually altering a behaviour, revolving around closer and closer approximations of the desired behaviour.

Anally pplcaton f Behavor

Behaviour analysis is a particularly effective tool for assisting children with autism spectrum disorders (Autm5) or developmental delays in acquiring and maintaining new skills. These treatment include the Lovaa Method and B (applied behaviour analysis) and utlize techn ue uch a decrete tral training. The fundamental principles of behavioural medicine are frequently adopted for use in educational settings, the workplace, and childcare.

How Broad Is The Population of Behavor naturally?

The application of behavior analy I very broad, ranging from attractng ndvual n overcoming drug adction to improvising the workplace for org Behavor analysis ha been appled to program related to det, exercise, juvenle deln uency, tolet training, education, kill ac

I'm nally Becoming More Widely Accepted?

Over the last 60 years, applied behaviour analysis has been recognized as the treatment of choice for behavioural problems associated with intellectual disability, autism spectrum disorder, or both. Many people also recognize that applied behaviour is capable of producing remarkable results in classroom learning. In recent year, interest in the field has grown rapidly outside the United States; B International now has over 5,000 members from nearly 50 countries and its affiliated chapters. memberhapp of approximately 13,000 worldwide.

What I ppled Behavor natually (ABA)?

The Scenery of ppled Behavor naly (B), an empirically validated or evidence-based approach to teachng using behavioural principles, law, and strategy, backed by over 60 year of reearch Typcally, B applied to teachng chldren, adolecent, and adult wth developmental disabilities, including UTM Spectrum Dorder (SD), learning disability, intellectual disability, behavioural disorder or challenge, special education, and mental health disorder. B can be ued to improve kill area or behavor and/or decreate maladaptve behavor that I ocally mportant for the famly and tude

Who Can Benefit From a People-Oriented Behavior-Based (B) Service?

ANY INDIVIDUAL WHO INVESTED IN Behavor change, whether kill ac uton or behavor reducton, INCLUDING PERSONS WITH Developmental DISABLITIES, can BENEFIT FROM Behavor n. The teachng procedure derved from our science can be appled to any natural envronment, INCLUDING homes. Special and general education classrooms, community-based activities, and therapy services such as Speech Therapy, Occupatonal Therapy, and Physical Therapy. B a data-driven cence that provides teachng tratege that result n measurable outcome for the consumer.

What Skills Can Be Acquired Through the Use of Behavioral Principles and Strategies if People Behaving Naturally?

- Numerous kill area can be added, such as:
- cademc skills such as reading, writing, and mathematics.
- Language Skills uch a re uettng, labelengthening, and

con_veration.

- hygene skills a tolettng, groomng, and dreng
- Ctvte of Daly LIVING (DL) klles uch as eating, meal preparation, and doing laundry.
- Communty kills, such as walking through a store, shopping, dining in a restaurant, or ordering a meal, and treet afety kills
- Socal knowledge includes developing relationships, communicating with others, blanding play, and learning appropriate social rules.
- Recreaton kills uch a ring a bke, wamming, learning to know, bowling, martial arts, and utilizing playground equipment.
- CREATIVE SKILLS uch art, pantning, and learning a musical instrument
- Technical knowledge uch as ung a computer, surfering the internet, and computer-baed actvte uch a vual art design.
- Copng klls emotonal regulation and elf-montoring.
- Where do I get rearch for suppporting treatment utilizing pplied Behavor nally?
- Please visit our link page to gain access to information about journals and books on behavioural analysis.

are there any onumer guidelines for hooting? nalyt behavior?
The UTM SpecIAL INTEREST GROUP (UTM SIG) developed a document to help guide consumers on the ualfcation of Behavior analysts to work wth children well. Consumers (parents or professionals) of behaviour analysis services may benefit from the information recommended in this document.

What Role Do I Have in Patent Treatment?
Ppled behavor analysts work n a variety of ettents, including home, workplaces, chool, and clnc. PatentS' treatment plan depends on theIR individual need, and B nterventon requer ure monitoring and continuous evaluation from eon to eon.

B therapists evaluate patents' behaviour to develop a treatment plan that will help them improve their communication and behavioural skills over time.

When B was first developed in the 1960s, it focused on a highly structured teaching system in which desired behaviour was broken down into specific components. The behaviour analyst would then guide the patient through an activity designed to teach the concept. The therapt rewarded the patent for each ucceful ACTIVITY COMPLETION. The patent repeated the procedure for each component of the behavior until the patent aembled all component nto a whole, modefed behavior

As B evolved, the procedure became less strenuous. Therapists choose their actions based on their patients' interests and interaction with their environment. The technique till utlizes the method of repeating and rewarding derable behaviour, but in a more fluid and natural manner. The approaches of behavor analysts have evolved dependent on the specific need of patient. These approaches can be divided nto two categorie: decrete trial training and natural envronment training.

1. Disreet tral training the more tradtonal behavor training approach that nvolve hghly structured one-on-one actvite where complex behavor I Once the patent ha learned the components, therapt them together until the patent can complete the entre complex behavioural task.
2. Natural envronment training occurs in a natural environment, such as a patient's home, workplace, or school. Therapists do not immediately begin training, but rather wait for the patient's natural nclnation and attempt to guide the therapy. Once patients express interest in a naturally occurring situation, therapists utilize graduated renforcement to elicit undesirable responses from them. This approach enable patent to employ the knowledge they learn in more generalized, day-to-day situations.

CHAPTER 5
Your Mind And The Way You Communicate

What is Effective Communication?
Effective communication entails more than simply exchanging information. It's about comprehending the emotion and intentions underlying the information. As well as being able to convey a message, you must also be able to write in a way that conveys the full meaning of what is being said and makes the other person feel heard and understood.

Effective communication sounded as if it should be ntnctve. However, all too frequently, when we attempt to communicate with another, something goes wrong. When we say one thing, the other person hears something else, and confusion, frustration, and conflict ensue. This can result in problem in your home. chool, and work relatenchenchenchenchenchenchenchenchenchenchenc

For many of us, communicating more clearly and effectively is a way to improve our communication skills. Whether you're attempting to improve communication with your spouse, child, boyfriend, or coworker, developing these skills can help you deepen your connections with others, build stronger trust and respect, and improve your performance.

Effective communication is one of the critical skills that one must possess to succeed in life. It is the foundation of any great and lasting relationship, whether personal or professional. Many people believe that communication is all about choosing the right words and saying what the other person wants to hear, but there is so much more to it. Communication can take many forms, and navigating them effectively can help u relate better wth other and find greater fulfillment in all ranges of our life. Continue reading for ntentonal method that can help you communicate more effectually with those around you.

What Is Keeping You From ommuncate effectually?

Common impediments to effective communication include the following:

1. **Strend utfontrol motiom**: When you are treed or emotonally overwhelmed, you are more likely to mread other people, send confuding or off-PUTTING nonverbal signals, To avoid confusion and misunderstanding, you can learn how to quickly calm down before continuing a conversation.

2. **Focusing lack:** You cannot communicate effectively while multitasking. If you're checking your phone, planning what you're going to say next, or daydreaming, you're almost certain to pick up on some nonverbal cues during the conversation. To communicate effectively, you must avoid distraction and maintain focus.

3. **Body Language Inconsistency**: Nonverbal communication should reinforce, not contradict, what is being said. If you say one thing but your body language says something else, your listener is likely to believe you are being dishonest. For example, you cannot say "yes" while hakeng your head no.

4. **Negative Body Language**: If you disagree with or doubt what is being said, you may use negative body language to rebuff the

other person's message, such as crossing your arms, avoiding eye contact, or tapping your feet. You do not have to agree with, or even like, what is being said, but to communicate effectively and avoid putting the other person on the defensive, it is critical to avoid ending on a negative note.

Effectve ommuncation Skill 1: Become agaged When we communicate with others, we frequently focus on what we should say. However, effective communication is less about speaking and more about listening. Lettenng well mean not jut undertanding the words or normal normal normal normal normal normal normal normal normal norma

There is a significant difference between engaged listening and simple hearing. When you're engaged wth what' beng

Additionally, you'll hear the subtle inflection in someone's voice that conveys how that person is feeling and the emotion they're attempting to communicate. When you are an engaged lener, you well not only better understand the other peron, but you well alo make that peron feel heard and understood, which can

By communicating in this manner, you will also experience a process that will reduce stress and support physical and emotional well-being. If the peron to whom you're talkng I calm, for example, ltening in an engaging manner will help to calm you a well. Similarly, if the peron agtated, you can help calm them by ltentvely and maken the peron feel undertood. If your goal is to fully comprehend and connect with the other person, lettenng in an engaging manner will frequently occur naturally. If it does not, try the following technique. The more you practice them, the more satisfying and receptive your interactions with others will become.

Tip For Becoming an Engaged Ltener

1. **Fully Focu n THE SPEAKER**: You cannot listen engagingly if you are constantly checking your phone or thinking about something else. You need to remember on the moment-to-moment experience to pck up the ubtle nuance and major

nonverbal cue n a converation. If you're having difficulty focusing on a speaker, try repeating their words in your head—it'll reinforce their message and assist you in remaining focused.

2. **Proud of our Right Ear**: trange all around, the bran's left deed contain the premary proceng center for both peech comprehenon and emoton. Because the left side of the brain is connected to the right side of the body, favouring your right ear can assist you in better detecting the emotional nuance of what someone is saying.

3. **avoid Attempting To Redrect The onveration To Your oncern:** By stating something along the lines of, "If you believe that's bad, allow me to tell you what happened to me." Not the same actual actual actual actual actual actual act attendentng to your turn to talk. You cannot concentrate on what someone else is saying if you are forming your own. Frequently, the peaker can read your facal expreon and know that your mIND' elewere.

4. **Demonstrate your interest in What' Beng Sad**: Nod occasionally mle at the peron, and make ure your poture open and inviting. Encourage the speaker to continue with brief verbal comments such as "yes" or "uh-huh."

5. **Try TO Set de The Final Judgment**: To communicate effectively with someone, you do not have to agree with their idea, value, or opinion. However, you do need to etade your judgment and wthhold blame and crtcm to explain them completely. When successfully executed, even the most difficult communication can frequently result in an unanticipated connection with someone.

6. **Deliver Feedback**: If there eem to be a deconnect, reflect what has been said through paraphrang. "What I'm hearing," or "Sounds like you're saying," are excellent ways to reflect. Don't merely repeat what the professor had verbatm, even if you feel nncere or unintelligent. Rather than that, express what the speaker's words mean to you. k ueton to explain certain

point: "What do you mean when you..." or "Is that what you're saying?"

Hear The Motive Behind The Word

It is the higher frequency of human speech that affects emotion. You can become more attuned to these frequencies and thus better able to understand what others are saying by exercising the tiniest muscle in your mddle e You can accomplish this by singing, playing a wind instrument, or listening to certain types of high-frequency music (a Mozart symphony or voln concerto, for example, rather than low-frequency rock, pop, or rock).

2nd Skill: Pay attention to nonverbal Signals

The way you look, leten, move, and react to another peron tell them more about how you're feelng than word alone can. Nonverbal communication, or body language, includes facial expressions, body movement and posture, eye contact, posture, the tone of your voice, and even your muscle tone and breathing. Developing the ability to comprehend and utilize nonverbal communication can assist you in connecting with others, expressing what you mean, navigating challenging situations, and developing stronger relationships at home. You can help effectIVE communcation by ung an open body language arm uncroed, standing with an open stance or setting on the edge of your eat

You can also utilize body language to emphasize or enhance your verbal meage by patting a friend on the back while complimenting him on his success, for example, or pounding your ft to underline your me

- Enhance How You Read Nonverbal Immunization 1. Be Aware of Individual Differences: People from different countre and culture tend to ue different nonverbal communcation geture, o it's critical to take age, culture, relgon, gende A mercan teen, a grieving woman, and a buneman, for example, are likely to utlize nonverbal gnal differently.

- Search for Nonverbal ommuncation Sgnal Group: Avoid reading too much into a single geture or nonverbal cue. Consider all nonverbal Anyone can help up occasionally and let eye contact go, for example, or brefly cro their arms without meaning to. Consider the gnal as a whole to obtain a more accurate "read" on a person.

Improve How You Delver NONverbal Immunization

1. **Utilize Nonverbal Signals That Correspond To Our Words Rather Than Attempting to Transform Them:** If you ay one thing but your body language ay something else, your lener well feel perplexed or suspicious that you're being duped. For example, sitting with your arm crossed and your head haken doesdododododon't mean that you agree wth what the other peron is saying.

2. **draft our Nonverbal Sgnal accordingly TO THE CONTENT**: For example, the tone of your voice hould be diferent when addreng a child than when addreng a group of adult. Simply, take the emotonal and cultural background of the peron you're nteractng with into account.

3. **vod Negative Body Language**: Instead, ue body language to convey positive feelings, even when you are not experiencing them. If you're nervous about a situation, such as a job interview, an important presentation, or your first date, for example, you can use positive body language to gain confidence, even if it's temporary. Rather than tentatively entering a room wth your head back, eye averted, and lading into a char, try tall wth your houlder back, many and m It will increase your self-confidence and assist you in putting the other person at ease.

3rd Skill: Maintain Street in check

How many tme have you felt treeded dure a dagreement wth your poue, kids, bo, frend, or coworker and then added or done omething yo If you can uckly releve tree and return to a calm state, you well not only avoid these regrets, but you well also help to calm the oth It is only when you are n a calm, relaxed state that you would be able to know whether the tate requre a repone, or whether the In situations such as a job interview, a business presentation, a high-pressure meeting, or an introduction to a loved one's family, for example, it's critical to manage your emotions.

Effectively communicate By Remaining Calm Under Preure

- Utilize tallng tactc to give yourelf tempt to thnk. Accept for a repeated ueton or for the clarification of a tatement before you respond.

- Paue to recommend your thoughts. While silence is not always a bad thing, paging can make you feel more in control than rushing your response.

- Make one point and provide an example or upport an example of normal normal normal normal normal normal normal normal n If your response I too long or you waffle about every point, you waffle longer the ltener's INTerest.

- Supplement one point wth an example and then gauge the lener' reaction to decide if you hould make another.

- Deliver your word. In many cases, how you say something is more important than what you say. Speak, maintain an even tone, and maintain eye contact. Maintain a relaxed and open body language.

- Wrap with an ummary and then top. Summarize your response and then top talking, even if the room ha a lence. You are not obligated to continue speaking to fill the lence.

Quick Stress Reference For effectual Communication

When a conversion begins to heat up, you need omething uck and medate to bring down the emotonal need. By learning to uckly reduce tre at the moment, you can affectly take tock of any trong emoton you're experiencing, regulate your fee

1. **Recognize When YOU ARE BECOMING STRESSED**: Your body well let you know if you are treed a you communicate. Is your musculature or tomach tight? Are your hands clean? How is your breath? Are you "forgetting" to breathe?

2. Take a moment to calm down before deciding to continue or potpone a converation.

3. **Bring OUR RESPONSE TO THE REQUEST**: The best way to relieve tre is through the eneght, out, touch, tate, mell, or movement. For example, you could put a pepperment on your mouth, ueeze a tre ball on your pocket, take a few deep

breath, clench and relax Each individual responds differently to each input, o you need to find a copping mechanm that oother to you.

4. **Seek Humor in the Situation**: When used appropriately, humour is an excellent way to alleviate tension when communicating. When you or those around you begin taking things too seriously, find a way to lighten the mood by sharing a joke or an amusing story.

5. **BE READY TO IMPROVE**: At times, if you can bend a little bit, you'll be able to fIND a happy maddle ground that reduce the tre level for everyone concerned. If you realize that the other person cares more about an error than you do, comprome may be easier for you and a good investment for the f

6. **Agree to disagree**, if necessary, and remove yourself from the situation so that everyone can calm down. If possible, take a walk outside or spend a few minutes meditating. Physical movement or fINDING a QUIET PLace to regard your balance can reduce treed ealy.

Skill 4: Asset Yourself

The drect, aertve expresion make for clear communication and can help boot your elf-eteem and decision-making knowledge. Being aeertve entails expressing your thoughts, feelings, and needs openly and honestly while standing up for yourself and respecting others. It does NOT imply being hostile, aggressive, or demanding. Effective communication is always about comprehending the other person, not about winning an argument or enforcing your opinion on another.

To improve Your ertvene:
- Assess yourelf and your option. They are vital to anyone else's.
- Recognize your need and desire. Learn to express them without impinging on the rights of others to expre negatve thoughts positively. It's acceptable to be angry, but you must also maintain a respectful demeanour.
- Receive feedback promptly. Accept commitments graciously, learn from your mistakes, and seek assistance when necessary.

- Acquire the ability to say "no." Recognize your LMT and don't let other take advantage of you. Seek alternatve to ensure that everyone feel good about the outcome.

Developing ertve ommuncation Techn ue

n empathetc aerton deliver entitlety to the other person. To begin, acknowledge the other person's situation or feeling, and then state your needs or opinion. "I understand you've been extremely busy at work, but I want you to make time for yourself as well."

scalalating aerton can be employed when your fresh attempts are failed. You get nearly freakly freakly freakly freakly freakly freakly freakly freakly freakly freakly freakly freakly frea For instance, "If you do not abide by the contract, I will be forced to pursue legal action." Practice aertvene in lower rake ter Alternatively, ask family or friends if you can practce aertvene techn on them first.

5 Ways To Improve Your Communication Skills

Communication is one of the most vital skills we can ever learn. It leads everything we do, whether we're communicating at work to meet deadlines and achieve results, or communicating with friends, family, and coworkers to build strong relationships. So many problem templetem templetem from poor communication, and it's unsurprising why. We are not taught how to communicate properly in school;

Something that we have to 'pck up' from the people around us. Unfortunately, unless we are fortunate enough to have a tellar communicator in our inner circle, we frequently pick up bad habits. I've made it my mission to learn a thing or two about communication, and I'll share a few key points with you today. One of the mortant, yet overlooked, skills of communicating th:

5 How to Improve Your Immune Capacity 1.

Never Speak vere People.

This demonstrates a genuine lack of regard. By speaking over someone about what you're saying, you're saying "I don't care what you're saying; what I have to say is more important."

2. Don't Complete the Sentence of other PEOPLE.

I used to do a lot of thinking when I did this. I want to helpfully fnhng people's entence for them. Wrong. The research ha hown that by doing that, you are d-empowering the other person becaue you are takenng control of the converation, o be

3. Paraphrase.

If you want to demonstrate that you have comprehended someone, then photography is an excellent tool. All you have to do is repeat back to someone what they have just said before you commit yourself. Here's an example: "So Barney, what I'm hearing is that the result are the number one objecve for you right now, and we need to find a fat oluton for you?"

4. Ctvely listen.

Concentrate on active learning rather than passive learning. The distinction is that while active listening entails engaging with and responding to another person based on what they have said, passive listening is simply the act of listening without responding.

5. Remember eye contact.

By looking the other person in the eye, you demonstrate that you are invested in what they are saying. Additionally, they keep you focused and le dtracted.

Tp For Effectve CommunICAtion Everyone ha her tyle of communication, but very few people have matered effectve communication. Breakdown n communcation occur all the tIME, with cone uence ranging from local problem, hurt feelings, and anger to dvorce and even volence. Understanding the psychology behIND good communcation can help u develop new habit, to get our meage acro more efficaciously. Effective Communication can be achieved by adhering to a few critical guidelines:

1. Establish et Mantan you contact

You contact play a crucial role in communication. Looking at another person I a way of regaining feedback at a particular point. Bran training helps you communicate and also ues an ynchronzengng gnal. People tend to look up at the end of their sentences, looking for feedback, and givenng their partner a chance to take over the There often I eye contact dure attempted nterruption, laught, and when anwerng hort ueton. Additionally, we look up at the end of grammatcal break. Hitchhikers, alepeople, charty-to haker, and other maximize eye contact to increase attention.

On the other hand, lack of eye contact, gnal embarrament (we look away to break the converation), punishment for bad behaver, or lac When people speak, they look at each other 75% of the time, but only 40% of the time when they listen. One wants to get and keep the attention of other. The often domnant, the bright, and the extrovert look more awkward when speaking than the often awkward.

2. Attempt To Send lear Message

There is a significant difference between simply saying something and saying something with intention. Say word that have meaning and would drive the point home. Keep the goal in mind – whether you're on a job interview, in a business meeting, or having a conversation with your partner. When you know where your word I going, your meage I much more lkely to come acro crytal clear.

3. be receptive to what other may may may may may may may Say Many of you go into converation communicating with your bran with a clear agenda of what we want. While it is beneficial to begin speaking and listening with a clear objective, remember to be adaptable. If they do not say exactly what you are expecting to hear – adapt. While they are speaking, nod, mumble, or make affrmate verbal noe (mmhmm, I concur). It helps to be an actve letener and not to tune out when the converation doesdodon't go your way. ven trying to understand what the other try to say or what they feel – regardless of whether your nterpretation I correct – enough to ncrease partner atf

4. Wat ForWat ForWat ForWat F THE ADDITIONAL Person To French

We all know one who want to talk wthout lettening; who eem to believe that what they have to say are facnatng to everyone ele around The best communicators understand that there is a kind of give and take between speaking and listening, a division of who is a speaker and who is a listener based on mutual respect and concern for each other.

Some people talk about themselves becaue they genuinely believe they are more nteretng than anyone else they know.

However, many people are overwhelmed by their feelings and push them away. In another way, monolog sends the incorrect message to your listener, whereas a two-way conversion brings people closer together. Never underestimate the value of effective communication. Frequently, people in management or with power a poltcan, doctor, or a tract mother are excellent communicators. Tend to your professional partner, give them signal that you are engaged, and message clearly. You will notice the difference.

CHAPTER 6
Truth And Relationship

How To SPEAK THE TRUTH n Relationshhip

I eech communcation a one of the better areas for ntmacy improvement. When need and feeling become unspoken, especially over long perod, fertle ground for mendertanding and feeling of health between the two precou people n a r Examples of what commonly results from not communicating our needs and feelings are reentment, a feeling of being misunderstood, the belef that our ne

Communicating our needs and feelings is a skill that many of us have never learned, but you can! Rather than communicating their needs and feelings plainly, many women: hold them in until they brew into rage and release in an emotional outburst. Keep an eye out for fear that expressing their needs and feelings will drive their partner away, and express their needs and feelings as demands rather than a declaration of clarity.

Take a moment to tune in to your thoughts—how do you intend to appropriately express your needs and feelings? If you can, also tune in to why you tend to supress or inadvertently expre them. Do you uppre becaue you are afraid that you wilt be dapponted wth her reponse when you tell her how you feel? Or were you taught during your upbringing that you should be napproprate and burdensome to others when you speak up? What behavour wa modeled for you in the department by your mother or mother fgure?

Now that we have deduced a few of the ways that no communcation, particular communcation, or demanding communcation can take the place of clear communcation, or d

A few good guidelines for clear and respectful expression. And when I say reSPECTful, I mean reSPECTful to your partner (not accuatory or demanding) ND, very importantly, reSPECTful to yourself. To let our body and heart tell us what we truly need and feel, and then to communicate this to our intimate partner, an act of self-honouring that grows our women's beauty every single day.

1. Do not asume: Don't assume that your partner knows how you feel if you've never expressed it with abolute, clear tatement. Because we tend to be highly intuitive, women communicate a great deal with one another through body language, gestures, and even tone of voice. Numerous men are not trong nterpreter of thee pave gnal and do not have to be!

2. Reflect on The Need Or Feeling You Want Your Partner To Understand: Before bringing it to the table wth your partner, be certain of what your core need or tatement to her. Ascertain that you are simply preparing to express your feelings or a desire to be fulfilled, and not that you are getting ready to off-load your feeling by accusing him of something. "I realized that after you told me you didn't want to attend my ter's graduation party with me, I felt disappointed and concerned that my family wasn't your property." I'd like to know what is true for you around here so that we can discuss it and both of our needs can be heard and hopefully met." Not acceptable: "You don't care about me or my family becaue you don't want to attend the graduation party. I need you to how up for event like thee, otherween you don't value me or the relatonhoch!"

3. Say it! : These guidelines are excellent preparation for you to say what you need and feel with clarity and room for your partner to respond in a way that is true for him. If you are expressing yourelf clearly and well without a tone of demand, and you always feel that your re uet are neglected or that your Some men (and, of course, women) are unwilling to lten.

to, APPRECIATE, HONOR, AND ACKNOWLEDGE the needS of their partner or other people in their life. As difficult as it may be, I encourage you to consider whether this is the type of person with whom you would like to spend your life.

In many way, thee gudelnee only cratch the urface of healthy communcation n relatonhology. However, if you follow them, you will really avoid many of the traps that lead u to feel un-een and un-heard, and maybe harmful or eve You will also begin to feel the transformative effect that clear communication has on relationships, which will increase. ntmacy and the wondreful knowledge that you are supported and loved.

I cannot overtate how poor communication can cause strut, reentment, and trepdation to speak honestly between partners. Especially when a man has been exposed to emotional outbursts, acceptance, and demands from his parent, he will grow guarded and independent from the woman who want him to come closer. One time that you can express your need clearly and wth pacoune for hm to reply truthfully, and you have already gained a large amount of h Two times, three times that you can do it, and you are truly beginning to build a relatonhip that can handle deep intimacy, truth, and secrecy.

The Power of Intmately SPEaking Our Truth Relationships

People assert that truth is subjective. It. People assert that the truth will set you free. and t does. People say many things about the truth but few speak it. Regrettably, the an enormous med opportunity for radcal and authentc elf-expreon. But what's worse is that we're not speaking our truth in a way that leads to deep and meaningful relationships. We do not recognize that by not speaking our truth, we deprive ourselves of what we most value: love.

How... here The Truth and Intuition

I find the truth distressing. It may not always be what I want to hear, but it always reaures in the end. To me, knowing the truth feels oozing and liberating. I am capable of dealing with whatever. I cannot deal wth the fear-inducing fgment of my magnaton when I'm telling myself that my intuition is off in the hope that I'm mistaken. We all have an intuition for a reason... Innate would alway would would would would would would would would would

'The only truly valuable thing Intuition.' lbert Einstein

I am not going into a philosophical debate about what 'truth' is or means. The truth is that we all live in segregated realities. Our realte template I contructed by our ue way of thinking. There can be one tuaton, but if there are six people involved, there will be six distinct stores. They are all valiant. They are all true. True for that individual. Each truth is valuable to me, and I value others' one-of-a-kind perception. I adore the subjectivity of it all. It's flowing and completely free.

When we believe that our parent is not being truthful with us, it can elicit a great deal of irrational thinking. Alternated thinking patterns of old attachment njure may get awoken. Jealou tendence can return to the surface. We may engage in unloving behaviours. When we feel removed from the truth, a great deal of irrational thinking arises, resulting in emotional distress. Something jut feel wrong. We are not at peace anymore. It is typically not the content of what is being kept from us, but rather the fact that something is being kept from us. Transparency nherent n truth. It's as if we can but the absence of it.

Truth Creates Space

The truth will set you free, they say, and it does. When I realize that my parent has told me the truth, I feel closer to him. I have the distinct impression that I am acquainted with him. There I safety in that. I may not always agree with what he has to say, but I am comforted by him being courageous and respectful enough to tell me. It makes it simple for me to trust him. and t lberaterateraterateraterateraterateraterateraterateraterateratera It appears that the more honesty and truth there are in our relationships, the more space we create. We experience true ntmacy and connection within that pace. When we are in the throw of irrate thinking, we become grapher and hold on for dear life. tghten and get retrcted. We struggle to breathe and to love. Because love necessitates space, which the truth provides.

"TRUTH = TRUTHFULNESS = SPACE = LOVe"
Truth CREATE TRUTH

When my parent tells me the truth, it increases my trust in him, his honesty, his integrity, and our relationship. He's telling me the truth, which keeps me safe. It keeps me safe from my irrational thoughts. It keep me affected from accurately funding out what he had been omitting, what he had had. Have truth and emotional safety for both partner.

The obverse of concealing honety and honety in relatonhip is paramount. It's vital. We are all aware that trust is necessary if we are to maintain a healthy and loving relationship. However, how can we expect truth if we withhold our truth? Or is it worse, if we are? How can we expect our partner to trust us if we do not provide the necessary conditions? When are we not honet?

If we speak our truth and are candid about who we are in relationships, How am I to believe that my parent truly loves me when I am unable to show him all of me? When I do not speak my truth? How am I to believe that he is making an informed decision? That have love for me really?

I am unable to. and that I why honesty or concealing our truth and thereby precluding a healthy, loving, and respectful relatonhoc dynamc from developing. When we choose to conceal ourselves or to lie, we choose fear. However, when we choose to share our truth, we choose honesty and love.

Truth Effort

When I speak my truth, I share myself with someone else. Sharing my truth compels me to open up, to be vulnerable. This is the place where the real connection happen. When I hare my entirety when I allow my

To earn to earn to I contribute. I CONTRIBUTE TO MYSELF. I devote my entire self to my partner and our relationship. Where I can be received. Where I can be accepted. This is where I can be loved. I am loved for who I am and what I am not. This is where we deal with what. This is where we love what we do. In the place, we exist as complete entte that choose to accompany each other within our own unue human experience. We prefer the truth a the basis for that. We choose love as the foundation for our lives.

Truth Re ure Action

We are ocal anmals, and as such, we communicate both verbally and non-verbally. That I where our ntuton comes from. Quite frequently, they don't have to be ad outrght. Some things we simply know. and once we know what we don't know, we know what we don't know becaue once we know, we canno longer deny the truth. and the truth necessitates action.

'Truth enables us to deal with whatever.' Tllhon Marlena

There may be truths that we do not wish to own, truths that we may feel ashamed of. However, we need to own them nevertheles. They are telling the truth. If we do not own them, they will eventually own us. We must be willing to face the consequences of our actions and inactions, our decisions and indiscretions, and our ndcreton. Simply because some truths are more desirable than others does not mean we can deny them. That would be a perfect full-blown denal. and there is no love in that.

u nert, pave, nactve denal leave. In denial, there I no moton. There wa no movement. There want to be any change. Life is a constant state of flux. Living in denal goes against the natural flow of life. It prevents you from acting. It top our general general general ge Dental is simply concealing something from ourelve. Denal lyng.

Being honest with ourselves, confronting our truth, and expressing it to the end of procratnation and avodance. We will return to life's natural flow. WE CONTINUE TO GROW.

What Is SPEaking Your Truth?

1. It Is Courageous To Speak Our Truth: It Is a bravery act to make ourelve vulnerable. It takes a special kind of courage to allow someone else to wtne it. We can open up to our vunerablity only when we deal wth our hame. The majority of people are too afraid to do that. Regrettably, the barrer to ntmacy and love I the barrer. By speaking our truth, we choose courage and love over the home.

2. It Is Respectful To SPEAK OUR TRUTH: It is respectful to provide our companion with all of the information contained here and to allow them to decide for themselves how they feel about us and whether they wish to be in a relationship with us. WE ARE RESPECTING theIR AUTONOMY and dere. By speaking our truth, we choose to respect and love over manipulation.

3. SPEAKING OUR TRUTH ELIMINATING: Le wegh down. u omn burden. The truth is libellous because we allowed the chip to fall. We top manipulating and controlling and open up to another experence. It I freedom. Finally, we allow for what to exist without struggle, denial, or persistence. By speaking our truth, we choose freedom and love over control.

4. SPEAKING OUR TRUTH & LOVING IT: When we speak our truth, we allow someone else to hear us. We allow them to become acquainted with us and choose to trust us. We make it poble for our partner to feel secure enough to open up and connect with u. Telling the truth enables ultimate intimacy. When we speak our truth, we choose ntmacy and love over Mabton.

5. SPEAKING YOUR TRUTHFULNESS nhancng: We make someone else special to you by sharing our truth with them. We create a special bond that enhances the connection we feel with them. We have something unusable for you. By doing so, we communicate to them how much we value them and how much they mean to us. By speaking our truth, we choose beneficence and love over Mabton.

6. SPEAKING OUR TRUTHFULNESS TRANSFORMATIVE: When we face our truth and take ownership of our experience, everything changes. WE STOPPed blaming. WE FINISH PUBLISHING. WE are top chang. Rather than that, we begin the process of opening to life by teepping out of our INTELLECT'S CONFINE. We become more comprehending, collaborative, and loving. We make a difference and have a positive impact on those around us. By speaking our truth, we choose growth and love over tagnation.

The Truth That I Gift

We cannot compel others to tell us the truth. We can only choose for ourselves whether or not to share our and with whom to share it. When we are with someone as willing as we are to share their truth, miracles occur. There are light and space, openness and truth, ease and connection. The truth is a gift to others, but only to ourselves. When we step into our truth and begin to open up, we begin to be honest with ourselves. We have to reevaluate pat choice. We have to make value value value value value valu We actually have a completely different experience wthout needing to change many thing outde. We allow ourelves a much richer and more frequent experience. One that tranforms u in such a way that touches others as well. and what's most lovely is that it's entirely dependent on one thing. One thing that is completely under our control, and no one else's: is our wilfulness to speak our truth.

Simple Relationship Truth You Require To Recognize

We all seek relatonhip and advice at some point or another. Whether we're initiating a new relationship or attempting to maintain an existing one, it's a safe bet that we have no idea what we're doing. Love I not something that we planned; mot often, we jut have to go along with it and fgure things out for ourelve. Every relationship is unique, and each problem requires a unique solution. That being said, there is a slew of bizarre relationship truths.

1. Relationships are not simple.

They necessitate work, time, and effort. They nvolve a lot of comprome. You need to have a doctor's demeanour and patience. That was a joke. Additionally, you need to have an energy of humor.

2. There Is No Use for "Fixing" What Isn't Broken.

Simply because something is not simple does not mean it is not good. To succeed in life and the business world, you must work tirelessly and consistently. You are not going to quit your job simply because you need to try. Similarly, you woulddodon't ut on a relatonhip jut becaue not all flowers and rainbows are flowers and rainbows.

Additionally, there is nothing wrong with being consistent. Allow yourself to be happy and don't be afraid of being comfortable. If there isn't a problem wth the relatonhp, don't go lookng for problems.

3. You Must First Love Yourself You want to love another Person.

How can you expect to genuinely love another person's ualte if you have trouble acceptng your own? Once you gain confidence in yourself, others will notice you more. When you accept yourself for who you are, you will be able to fully appreciate and comprehend the best qualities of others.

4. You Cannot Love Someone If you like Nobodies.

Maintain an open mind when meeting new people. Do not shut everybody out immediately. The world ha o much to offer, and you won't experience any of it if you refer to venture outside your comfort zone. At times, feeling uncomfortable is beneficial. As with love, people will astound you.

5. A BALANCE OF ntmacy AND SPACE IS REQUIRED.

Demonstrate interest in your gnfcant other's hobby and work, but refrain from intruding. Thus, invite him/her into your world. Spend time together, but avoid making it seem as if you always need to be together to be happy. Share information about yourself that you would not ordinarily share: your tore, your apraton, your fear. Make yourverable. Encourage your companion to do the same. Listen.

6. Immunity Is Paramont.

Be on the same page as your partner, or at the very least on the same chapter. I wanted to have a relatonhip where my grrlfrend and I were very different book. corney at order, honety the best policy. Be honet to yourelf and to your partner.

7. arguing healthy.

You and your partner are not going to agree on everything, and that is perfectly normal. The envy of healthy arguing necessitates that you both understand how to debate these points and understand each other's perspectives. Be mature and admit when you're wrong, and accept the fact that not everyone shares your opinion.

8. People vary.

This is something you have no control over. It is critical to ACCEPT theSE TYPES OF THINGS and worry about what you can CONTROL, about the progre you make.

9. Relationships not Projected.

Individuals may change, but you should not enter a relationship to change someone. It never work the way you planned, which means you don't truly love your partner for who he/she is.

10. Once heater, always heater.

If he cheated on his ex-girlfriend with you, what makes you believe he won't cheat on you with someone else? True, people change, but moral not jut appear out there. When you embark on a relatonhology wth omebody, you hould have an idea of what you are getting yourelf into.

11.You Should Not "Remain Friends."

This is a mistake that many couples make when a relationship comes to an end. Everybody know what that means: one peron doesdodon't want to cut the other peron completely out of his/her life, and the other peron thinking: "weome. We'll be friends for a while and then reunite within a month." This is always a bad idea for everyone, and it frequently results in hatred. way to elect out of communcation.

12. HATE LEAVE Brue, BUT LOVE LEAVE Scar.

The sensations of hatred and corn are uually temporary. However, the damage that love can do to a person is frequently much more permanent. Lot love ha become a part of u; a mark we wear every day that remember u of our part and all of the learned. On the plus side, that "damage" can be a favorable type of permanent. My parents have been in a loving marriage for over thirty years, and they most assuredly have the car to prove it.

13.Relationships are similar to Shoes.

Some look tylh outder, but only the peron wearng them know the pain they bear nede. Walking in a new neighbourhood is similar to meeting a new person—unfamiliar at first, but as you break them in, you develop a sense of security. You reach that comfort zone n whch you regularly need to unteeth.

You outgrow ome hoe. Some become wronned out. Some caue pain or leave you exposed. You can wear ome hoe anywhere. Certain shoes become drippy, and when you wear them, you can't remember where they've been. You hesitate to throw away some hoe. Certain individuals wear hoes until they are soulless.

Learn From Of course, we all wish there wa jut one simple truth about relatonhhp. There isn't one. The very relationships in which we partake will teach us something new about ourselves, as well as about other people. This experience wilt ultmately lead u to the ready drecton, hopefully to one who wilt accept, and support.

CHAPTER 7
Confidence And How It Is Displayed

What Exactly Is Self-Confidence?

Self-confIDENCE an attattude about your knowledge and ablte. It means you accept and TRUST yourSELF and have an energy of control over your life. You know your trength and weakne, and have a potential vew of yourelf. You get realtc expectation and goal, communicate effectively, and can handle crtcm. Self-confidence is not a self-motivating perspective. It is a judgment about capable for the accomplishment of one goal, and therefore, but be considered within a broader conceptualzation of motivation that provides

On the other hand, low self-confidence may cause you to experience self-doubt, be passive or submissive, or have difficulty trusting others. You may feel neglected, unloved, or sensitive to crtcm. Confidence in yourelf may depend on the textuation. For instance, you can feel extremely confident in one area, such as academics, but lack confidence in others, such as relationships.

- Having a high or low level of self-confidence is rarely related to your actual abilities and is mostly determined by your perception.Percepton are the way you thnk about yourelf, and they can be flawed.

- Low self-confidence may stem from a variety of experiences, such as growing up in an unsupportive and critical environment or being separated from your friend or family for the first time. Individuals with low self-esteem frequently make cognitive errors.

Self-onfdence TYPE

Occasionally, however, we get a little confused about what type of confidence we are talking about.

Do we mean the brah cocknel that teenage boy deplay when they predect how many goal they will cruh their opposition by?

Do we mean the confidence we feel when performing a skill that we've practised numerous times in the past? Or rely on an even more multifaceted psychological treatment?

'Be confident' is such generc advice that it is exceedingly useful. For a change, let's consider the various types of self-confidence, from least to most beneficial.

1. 'Unwarranted' offence

lo known a cocky arrangement. This is our teenage boy example from above. You can be confident when, in fact, you should not be. This type of confidence stems from one or both of the following:

Overestimating your abilities
- Recognize your adversaries or the magntude of the take n from you
- Neither of these is a good thing. It almost always fails, and if you were unlucky enough to brag about the outcome in advance, it could be a very humiliating failure.

Unwarranted confidence I expectally dangerou when the peron welding it a poton of power. Consider the C.O. who believes he is infallible and makes risky investment decisions. Or the fghter who lam h opponent n the meda only to find helm lammed when the time comes to get on the rng. To avoid it, seek out brutally honest feedback about your true abilities. Inquire of those who have tackled the same challenge what it really looke like. Stay away from people who give you unrealtc praise — it may feel good at the time, but you will regret it when your unwarranted confidence and an inflated ego are severely punctured in the future (parents are hardly punctured).

2. Poted in' onfidence

There was a time when our self-help guru advised us to go to the mirror every morning and tell ourselves with conviction phrases such as 'I am amazing', 'nobody can beat me, and 'I can do it. Let's name the pated on confidence. We don't feel confident deep down, but we're attempting to build a thick layer of confidence on top of our doubts. It's fairly self-evident that pated on confidence can crack an egg — it certainly isn't relent or endurant.

However, it can be mldly ueful as the mpetu for initiating something difficult or performing a task for the first time.

Consider a first-time act in the chool play for students who suffer from tage fight. Telling herelf 'I can do that' may be the main extra push he needs to take a couple of teeps from the wing to the spotlight. The same holds for the gymnast who is terrified of attempting a new skill on the beam. A lttle pated on confidentiality may help her try the trck for the first tme.

Following that, the third type of confidence can kck n.

3. 'I've already DONE it' infidelity

Once you've done something, you'll automatcally have more confidence the second time around. and by the hundredth time you've accomplished it, you've forgotten about the doubt you had at the start. It may have become automatc to the extent that you've reached a level of unconcou competence. Driving a car is an excellent example. Your first tempt behIND the weel, you are likely to ue the maximum amount of brainpowder not required to focu on the gear, braking, and oncoming traf Six months later, you are nang along to the rado, chatting with your friend at the paenger eat, and not even thinking about how to change gear. You're supremely confident in what you're doing because you've done it numerous times previously.

As an athlete, if you've previously won a competition, don't you feel more confident about competing in the same event the following year? You already know that you are good enough to win. And the ame goe for kill – the first time you attempt something difficult and lack confidence. However, with each repetition, your self-confidence grows. It may appear to be the most authentic type of confidence. However, it only listed the third most useful type of self-confidence because, while it is beneficial for repeating what we have already done, it does not assist us in growing. For that, we require the fourth kind.

4. Effort Will Result In Result' onfidence

This is the most beneficial type of confidence because it is the fuel that rescues us from not being able to do something, to manage it. This type of confidence instils a certainty that if I work diligently, I will eventually achieve what I've set my sights on. Sport a high-risk endeavor.

Many, many children begin with the dream of playing professionally or making the Olympics. Very, very few of these children do. The one that ha the type of confidence that all have. an unwavering belief that effort and time will result in success.

The ame hold true for all the most accomplished people in any indutry. In-born talent and overnght ucce are both myths that make a good story in the meda but are utterly untrue. The truth is that all successful people have put in thousands of hours of work and bridged the gap from beginning to end with the confidence that my effort, sustained over time, will result in.

This is an excellent word to incorporate into your vocabulary when considering your goal and skill development 'yet'. The tiniest word teaches your bran to develop the type of confidence at mple that ucce will happen, jut han't happened yet.

- 'I haven't learned how to do that kill yet.' (however, I will mater it)
- 'I have not yet won a competition at that level.' (however, I will in time)

- 'I haven't figured out how to solve that type of problem yet.' (but with enough effort, I'm sure I'll figure it out)

The final type of confidence I balanced on the long term. It manifests itself when you realize that the extra time you invested in studying resulted in a higher grade. It develops when you execute a difficult trick flawlessly.

You've been late to practice at occer training. It grows when you struggle to letten to and ncorporate your coach's feedback, even when it's difficult. It flourishes when each day, week, month, year, and decade of effort accumulate to yeld a major vctory.

Self-confidence. We all desire it. and we've probably all received some useful advice on the occasion. Perhaps the guide will assist you in identifying the more beneficial type of confidence and assisting you in building and developing it. Keep n memory to:
- refute the arrangement of 'unwarranted' confidence
- Utilize 'pasted on' confidence sparingly, and only to entice you into taking that ntal, carry tep forwar.
- Avoid becoming too comfortable in the confidence of 'I've already done it,' or you'll be compelled to improve.
- Delberately cultivates the most beneficial type of confidence – a certainty that 'effort and time will lead to results'.

How To Increase Your Self-Confidence
- Recognize and emphasize your strength. Reward and PRAISE YOURSELF for your effort and progress.
- When you tumble on an obtacle, treat yourelf well. Avoid relying on failure.
- Establish realtc and achievable goals. Expect perfection; it is impossible to be perfect in every aspect of life.
- Slow down when you are emoted and thnk logcally about the emotion.
- Challenge makeng aumpton about you, people, and tuation.
- Recognize that previous negative life experiences do not dictate your future.
- Expreience your feelings, beliefs, and need drectly and respectfully

- Learn to say no to irresponsible re-use.
- Individual counselling can also help you boost your self-confidence if you require additional assistance.

Why is confdence uch an emportant Thing?

Confidence is believing in yourself, feeling secure in your true self, and knowing your worth. When you are confident, people believe you; confidence is attractive, brings success, helps you connect well with others, and you generally feel happier. Only you can assert that you are not confident. What excuse do you have toppng you from your self-confidence?

How to Gain Confidence & Maintain It
- Positivity main chatter & belief you're a good peron
- Learn to learn to learn to learn to learn to learn to learn to learn to learn to learn
- Be social
- Exit your comfort zone and have a go
- Maintain a goal-oriented mindset and be proud of your accomplishments.
- accept complements
- Do the best you can at
- Consider yourself and recognize that you are a good person.
- Spol yourelf
- Clean & tidiness
- Accept that you and others are not perfect; that you make mistakes; but accept responsibility.
- Be jubilant and aware that you require it
- take note of who you are
- Carry out what you love
- not put thing off
- Have grattude
- Be a kind person
- Seek forward to life and the future
- Consider that you are n control and have the power to change thing
- Search for alternations to challenges and methods to acheve

uccess

- encourage the people around you & respect their vew
- Respect your vew & aertvely stand for yourelf

HOW TO LOSE CONFIDENCE

- Not affect your preentation
- Feel unhappy and do something to keep you merable
- Be a judge of yourelf or other
- Feel as if you're not as good as another?
- Do not believe in yourelf & demonstrate yourelf
- Consider your future hopele.
- Consider & hear the negative
- Take something and people for granted
- Accuse yourself
- never take responsibility, feel orry, or blame anyone else
- Feel tred & lazy all the time
- Do not ocalze
- Punish or despise yourelf
- 'Str over' a bad thing, feel alone and unloved
- Lten to any other negatve chatter and good about you

What Am I Confident In?

Confidence mean feeling secure about yourelf and your ability not in an atypical way, but in a genuine, secure way. Confidence is not about feeling superior to others. It's an uet nner knowledge that you are able to have. Confidence is a state of being clear-headed about whether a hypothesis or prescription is correct or whether a particular course of action is the best or most effective. Confidence derives from the Latin word fdere', which means "to trust"; thus, having self-confidence entails having trust in one's self.

In this context, arrogance or hubris refers to unfounded confidence in something or someone, believing they are capable or correct when they are not. Overconfidence or presumptuousness exaggerates belief in someone (or something) that is succeeding, without regard for failure. Confidence can be a self-fulfilling philosophy, as those lacking it may fail or refrain from attempting due to a lack of it, while those who possess it may succeed due to their possession rather than due to a lack of it.

The concept of self-confidence is frequently used to refer to a person's judgment, ability, and power, among other things. One's self-confidence grows as a result of the experience of completing a specific action. It is a positive belief that one can do so in the future.

generally do what one where to do. Self-confdence I not the ame a elf-eteem, where an evaluation of one' worth, where elf-confdence more pecifcally truth on one' a Abraham Malow and many other have emphazed the need to dengue between elf-confidence a a generalized peronalty characteristic, and elf-confidence co Self-CONFIDENCE typICALLY refers to general SELF-CONFIDENCE. This is distinct from self-efficacy, which mythologizes. Albert Bandura defined a 'belief in one's ability to succeed in a specific situation or accomplish a task, and thus the term more accurately refers to pecific elf-confidence. Pychologists have long noted that a person can express the confidence that he or she can complete a specific task (elf-efficacy) (e.g. cook a good meal or write a good novel) even though self-efficacy required to complete a specific task (e.g., write a novel). However, theSE TWO TYPES OF SELF-CONFIDENCE are correlated wth each other, and for that reason, can be ealy CONFLUENCE.

Confident Individuals:
- Feel secure rather than insecure
- They know they can rely on their knowledge and trength to handle whatever come up.
- Feel prepared for daily challenges such as tests, performances, and competitions.
- Consider I can" rather than I can't."

Why Does Confidence Matter?

Confidentiality help you feel ready for life's experience. When we are confident, we are more likely to move forward with people and seize opportunities, rather than retreat from them. And if something does not work the first time, confidence enables you to try again. It's the inverse when confidence is low. Individuals who lack confidence may be more prone to try new things or reach out to new people. If they fail at

They may be le likely to try again if they do something the first time. Lack of confidence can help people reach their full potental.

Believing in Yourself

Has anyone informed you that you are mart? Funny? Kind? Artistic? an excellent tudent? an excellent writer? an excellent athlete?

When people prae u or recognize our knowledge and capabilities, it can boot our confidence as long as we beleeve these good things, too. If you've ever questioned the positive things people say about you, that's the inverse of self-confidence. To truly feel confident, you must believe that you are capable. The bet method to get that belef I to utilize your knowledge and talent by learning and practcing. Confidence help u move forward to develop and decorate our capablete. When we see what we are capable of and commit to our objectives, confidence grows even stronger.

How To Increase Your Confidence

Everybody can work to gain more confidence. Here are a few tips to get you started:

1. Cultivate an onfdent MINDSET: When your ner voice says "I can't," redirect them to say "I can." Alternatively, you could say, "I am aware that I am capable of learning (or doing) if I apply my mind to it."

2. KINDLY Compare Yourself: It's natural to compare ourselves to other people. It's a method for us to understand ourselves and develop the ualte we admre. However, if comparison frequently leaves you feeling bad about yourself, it's a good idea to work on your confidence and self-esteem.

3. Eliminate Self-Doubt: When we have doubts about our ability, we feel inferior, unworthy, or unprepared. That can make u avoid people and situations that we may enjoy and grow from.

4. TAKE A SAFE RISK: Sign up for a school committee,

volunteer to assist with a project or bake sale, or look for a team or talent how.

Rae your hand in cla more frequently. Speak to that cute kd next to your cence cla.

5. CHALLENGE YOURSELF To Do SOMETHING OUTSIDE our Normal Comfort Zone: Make a note of something you'd like to do if only you had more confidence. Give yourself a little push and do it. Now that you've done that, pick something else to try and repeat the proce. Confidence grows with every step forward.

6. Recognize Your Talent and Assist Them in Shining: We were taught to work diligently to improve our weaknee. Certain things are critical, such as raising a bad grandparent. However, don't let working on a weekend prevent you from becoming even better at what you're already good at.

7. Carry out our Homework: Study. Agnment. Prepare for cla, tet, and uzze. Why? If you've kept on top of classwork all along, you'll feel more confidant during tests and finals. The best defene againt tet anxety and chool tre to keep up and do the work regularly.

8. DARE TO BE THE TRUE You: Allow other to ee you for whom you make, necurte, and all. When we don't feel that we have to have to have to have to have to have to have to have to have to have to have to ha Embrace your uniqueness rather than attempting to be someone else or acting in ways that are not true to you.

Six Ways to exude Confidence
No one feel confident 100% of the time. People have bad days or encounter obstacles they weren't expecting, and it can knock them off their feet. Others have a shaky belief in confidence and believe they cannot be confident because they have previously failed or made mistakes. You do not have to be confident all the time, but you can learn how to appear confident when necessary.

Confidence is not something you have; it is something you create. It's an ene of certainty. It's the conviction that you can accomplish anything that comes your way. It's a state of mind that you can cultivate to assist you in obtaining the outcome you desire. If you aren't

Confident, you don't always have to put yourelf through a pep talk to get pyched up. Rather than that, learn how to appear more confident simply by utilizing your body to your advantage.

Confdence eluve omewhat. You understand that you must be confident if you wish to make a positive impact in the professional world, but acquiring that confidence is not as simple as it appears. For some, confidence comes naturally, but for the majority, it's more difficult to achieve— especially in unfamiliar situations or with unfamiliar people. Assure yourself that you are not alone, and keep in mind one critical fact about confidence: In most situations, it is irrelevant whether you feel confident on the inside as much as it is that you appear confident on the outside. The goal is to appear confident, even if you are not, and there are numerous tricks you can use to accomplish this.

Learn How To Appear More Confidential & Feel More Confidential

Many people believe they must first feel confident before they can work on how to increase their confidence. The converse may be true. We've all heard the clché phrase "fake it til you make it," but in this case, it's true. Fake confidence by holding a power tance, putting a relaxed expression on your face, and holding your head high. You will not only look more confident but also feel more confident, by posing your body in this manner. If you find yourself uncertain or anxious in a new situation, learning how to appear more confident can alleviate some of your fear and assist you in handling the situation with grace. Learning how to appear confident while becoming more confident is a winning strategy that will assist you in achieving your goal more quickly.

The Importance of Looking and Feeling Secure

Learning how to look more confident and feeling that confidence are critical components of achieving your goal. Without confidence, you will lose your edge in negotiations, develop unproductive habits, and struggle to build and maintain healthy relationships. If you lack self-confidence and lack a strategy for demonstrating it, you will be unable to create empowering beliefs.

consider your potential and future. Confidence leads to better job opportunITIES and promotes and tronger parenting knowledge and deeper connection wth other. If you lack confidence in yourself or cannot appear confident, the people in your life will not believe you or rely on what you say.

Target Tall

Take up space by standing tall. Maintain your shoulders back and your pne traght. This way Individuals who louch or minimize their body tend to be very unconfident or uncertain. You can also practice the "power pose" technique before entering the room by extending your arm far above your head or by placing your hand on your hip with your elbow wide. These "power poe" have been expermentally proved to reduce Confidence, but you may look a lttle lly dong them dure your event, o keep them a prelmnary rtual.

The Efficacy Of Body Language

Your body language is the very first thing that someone notices about you. If you have a terrible poture and your head down, people won't thnk you're a confident peron. Nobody looks at someone with their arm crossed over their chest and their gaze fixed on the ground and thinks, "That person appears confident and knows what they're doing." Fortunately, how to appear more confident through body language can be learned. Here are some tips on how to convey confidence through body language.

dreserve Your Posture

The number one fact that make you appear le confident? Poor potent. Standing lumped over or with your houlder caved in can make you look unnatural. Rather than allowing your body to hunch over, stand up straight, hold your head up high, and push your shoulders back. ddtonally, when you're particularly .

Someone, t help to have your body facing ther drectly. When determining how to appear more confident, always remember to begin by adjusting your posture; everything else will fall into place.

Put an End to Your Fidgeting

Practising how to appear confident when your nerves kick in can appears to be a daunting task. Nervou energy can often lead to fdgetting to releave document or anxety. Fdgetting nclude warning your hand, bouncing your foot, or tapping your finger or a pencl againt a table. While that may help elminate some nerves, it also makes you look unprofessional and uncomfy. If you notice yourself fidgeting during a new encounter or while delivering a presentation, take a moment to regroup. Take a deep breath to assist yourself in relaxing and attempting to remain in the present moment. If your hand are fdgettng, place them on your lap or flatter them together o they are no longer a dtracton. After repeating this several times when the urge to fidget is strong, you'll be able to continue getting together.

Examine Your Hands

The way you hold your hand is a critical aspect of how to appear confident. Wrnging your hand, folding your arm, or tckeng your hand n your pocket give off nervou or uncomfortable energy to everyone ar If you're unsure what to do with your hand while speaking or listening, try a simple gesture that exudes power and certainty in what you're saying: the hand teeple. Make a teeple happe wth your hand by placing the teeple tips of your finger together to form a point. If you're wondering how to convey confidence, this is an excellent gesture that can be used in a variety of situations, whether you're delivering a presentation or deeply listening to someone else.

Invest your time in your contact

Drect eye contact let people know you're focung your attention on them and a techn you ue with high return when workng on how to However, makeng an excessive amount of ntene eye contact

can be affective, o you hould am for a happy medum. The 80/20 rule is a good rule of thumb. Meet your partner's eye 80 per cent of the time you're speaking and allow your eyes to wander or focus on something else for the remaining 20%. Making eye contact at critical points during the conversation with the person to whom you're speaking not only makes you appear more confident but also demonstrates your friendliness and empathy.

Enhance Your Handshake

Meeting new people can often generates anxiety, but if you're able to work on how to appear confident in public, you'll project a better image and distract yourself from any nerve. When meeting someone, especially in a professional setting, the first point of contact is frequently the handshake. ualty handhake can enhance the tone of your nteraction. You want to firmly grasp their hand, but not too tightly. Some professional recommend "ANCHORING" the handhake, or ung your other hand to offently touch the peron' outtretched arm betwe This demonstrate authentcy and care, and can be a good way to form an instant connection.

Maintain Consciousness Of Your Facial xpressions and Voce

While body language plays a significant role in determining how to appear more confident, keep in mind that your voice and expression also play a significant role. Happy people are perceved as more confidant and relaxed, makeng puttng a mle on your face a uck and easy fx when fonding a way to eem confid The tone and nflecton of your voice are also critical. When you mle, your voice will naturally sound more pleasant and confident. Additionally, make a point not to rae your ptch at the end of entence, as that can make teem like you're asking for ueton or looking for approv

In term of content, the word you ue make a sizable difference in how confidant you appear to other. Stammering, ung hetant words such as "maybe," and decreang a tready or worred feeling can be damageful or worred feeling can be damageful

interactions. Speak positively and with conviction about how other, you are secure and confident in your environment.

Select Big Step

One comes into play when you enter, exit, or move around a room. Take wede, urefooted steps with every move, rather than uck, hurred, or frantc steps. Avoid being hurried to get anywhere, and remember to keep your body posture aligned. This slow, deliberate series of movements will make you appear confident, so much so that people several yards away from you will be able to pick up on it.

The wonderful thing about pretending to be confident is that you will eventually track yourself down to being confident. As with proper posture and conversational manners, the only thing preventing you from successfully implementing these strategies is your inability to do so consistently. The more you practice appearing confident, the more naturally it will come to you, and the more confident you will appear and feel. With your newfound confidence, you'll be able to speak more artfully, command a more attentive audience, and be viewed with greater respect by your peers.

CHAPTER 8
How To Fake Your Body Language

Faking powerful Body language

People wth powerful body language movement that tend to be more open and pread out, and take up more space, alo feel confident. They are more likely to take risks, feel optimistic, and even produce less cortisol (the stress hormone) and more testosterone (the dominance hormone). Though we've known for a long time that expressing dominance through bodily language contributed to a more powerful appearance, Cuddly discovered that lower levels of stress were also a significant contributing factor. She and her partner broughed people to a lab and aked them to adopt both HGH- and low-power poe to find out if mere faking confidence (and d The study discovered that while faking high-power levels increased people's confidence and willingness to take risks, their testosterone levels increased and their control levels decreased significantly. In vertue, low-power poe cause the exact inverse reaction.

The information is enticing in a lab, but it means nothing if it cannot be put into practice in real life. The study's findings indicate that you may wish to prawl out in a stressful situation to feel more powerful, but kcking your feet up during, say, a job interview will lead you in the wrong direction. Cuddly explain that it isn't the body language during high-tre moment that matters, but rather the nonverbal gnal gnal you create pror. In the event of a job ntervew, he discovered that opening up your body for a few mnute pror even if it's privately n the bathroom can mak

Some people may take issue with the concept of "fake it til you make it" because they don't want to feel like a freak all the time, but Cuddly explains that it's more of a process of faking.

Feeling powerful and confident is a process and something you can learn. It begins with a minor adjustment to your body language, something that anyone can do.

How To READ Body Language – Disclosing The Secrets Behind

Nonverbal Common Cues Whether you are at the office or out with frends, the body language of the people around you speaks volume. It has been suggested that body language accounts for more than 60% of what we communicate. To learn to read nonverbal cues, individuals acquire a valuable skill.

From eye behaviour to the direction in which a person points his or her feet, body language reveals what a person is thinking. The following are valuable tips to assist you in learning how to read body language and better understand the people with whom you interact. READ the ENTIRE ARTICLE to learn all eight common body language cue.

Study the eyes

The eye Body Language: Your behaviour can be quite telling. When communicating with someone, pay attention to whether he or she maintains direct eye contact or looks away. The inability to maintain direct eye contact can result in boredom, distraction, or even deception – especially when someone looks away and to the side. On the other hand, when a person looks down, it frequently results in nervousness or ubmvene. lo, check for dated people to determne if anyone report favorably toward you. Puple dlate when cogntve effort reduces, o if one focued on one or onething they lke, theIR puple will dlate automatcally. Although pupl dlaton can be difficult to detect, you should be able to do so under the right circumstances.

The banking rate of a person can alo explain volume about what I happening nexternally. When people think more or are treed, their blinking rate increases. In some cases, increased blinking rate and created lying – especially when accompanies by touching the face (particularly the mouth and eye). Glinting at something can imply a direction for that thing. For instance, if omeone glances at the door, that may indicate a desire to leave. Glancing at a person can imply a desire to speak with him or her. When it comes to eye behaviour, it is also recommended that looking upward and to the right dure converation ndcate a le habeen told when looking upward and to the left ndcate the peron tellng the truth. The reason for this is that people look up and to the right when they are concocting a story, and up and to the left when they are recalling an actual memory.

Gaze t Body Language – Face Mouth Touchng r Small

FACE BODY Language: Although people are more likely to control their facial expressions, you can still pick up on critical non-verbal cues if you pay close attention. Pay particular attention to the mouth when attempting to decipher nonverbal behaviour. Simple mle body language attraction techn ue can be a major geture. Smiling is a critical non-vegetarian cue to watch for. There are variou type of mle, including genuine mle and fake mle. A genuine mle engage the entire face, whereas a fake mle ue only the mouth.

The genuine mle suggests that the peron I happy and enjoyng the company of the people around her or her. On the other hand, fake mles are not intended to convey pleasure or approval, but rather to imply that the mler is feeling something else. "Half-mle" I another common facial behavior that engages only one degree of the mouth and ndcates arcam or uncertanty. Additionally, you may note a light grmace that lats le than an econd before someone melle. The typcally suggested that the peron had her or her datafacton behIND a fake mle. Tight, pured lp also ndcates dpleaure, while a relaxed mouth ndcates a relaxed attitude and a positive mood. Covering the mouth or tuching the lp with the hand or finger when preaching may be an andcator of lyng.

Pay ttenton To roxmty

eye Body Language Proximity: I the detachment between you and the other person. Pay attention to how close someone stands or sits next to you to determine if they view you favourably. Standing or tang cloe to one may be one of the better ndcator of rapport. On the other hand, if omeone back up or move away when you move near, that could be a in that the connection I not mutual. You can tell a lot about the type of relationship two people have simply by observing their proximity. Keep in mind that some cultures prefer less or more distance during an interaction, and that proximity is not always an accurate indicator of affinity with someone.

See f you Involve makeng the body language of the other peron. When interacting with someone, check to see if the other person mirrors your behaviour. For example, if you're sitting at a table with someone and place an elbow on the table, wait ten seconds to see if the other person does the same. Another common mirroring gesture entails taking a sip of a drink at the same time. If someone mmcs your body language, that a very good in that he or he I trying to establish a rapport wth you. Change your body posture and observe whether other people do the same.

Observe THE HEAD Body Language: Movement ye The peed at which a person nods their head while you speak and communicates their presence – or lack thereof.

Slow nodding indicates that the person is engaged in what you're saying and wishes for you to continue speaking. Fat nodding ndcate the peron has enough heard and wants you to finish speaking or give hm or her a turn to speak. Tilting the head deway down dure converation can be a sign of nterest n what the other peron ayeng. Tilting the head backward can be a general of upcon or uncertainty. Additionally, individuals point with their heads or faces at individuals they are interested in or share an affidavit with. In group and meetings, you can tell who the people wth power are by how frequently people look at them. On the other hand, the le-gnfcant people are le-gnfcant people are le-gnfcant people are le-gnfcant people are le-gnfcant people are

Consider the ther eron' Body Language: Feet yes area of the body where people often "leak" valuable nonverbal cue next to the feet. The reason people unintentionally communicate nonverbal messages through their feet is that they are typically so preoccupied with controlling their facial expression and upper body positioning that critical clues are missed. va feet. When a person is standing or sitting, they will generally point their feet in the direction they wish to travel. If you notice that someone's feet are positioned in your direction, this can be a good indication that they have a favourable opinion of you. This applies to both one-on-one and group interaction. You can learn a great deal about group dynamics simply by observing the body language of the people involved, particularly the direction in which their feet are pointing.

Additionally, if someone appears to be engaged in conversation with you, but their feet are pointing in the direction of someone else, he or she will most likely speak to that person (reg).

Watch For Hand Signals
Hand Body LanguAGE: As with the feet, the hands reveal critical nonverbal cues when examining a body language. This is a critical tip when reading body language: pay close attention to the next paragraph. Maintain body language hands in the pocket while standing. Look for particular hand gnals, such as another person putting their hand in their pocket or putting their hand on their head. This can ndcate anything from nervoune to outral deception. Unconcou pontng ndcated by hand geture can alo peak volume. When makeng hand geture, a person will point in the general direction of the person they share an affinity with (thee nonverbal cue are expectally major to watch for during mee).

Supportng the head wth the hand by retaining an elbow on the table can indicate that the peron I lettenng and holdng the head to focu On the other hand, supporting the head with both elbow on the table can ndcate boredom. When a person hold an object between her or her and the peron they are nteractng with, they erve a a barrer, meaning to block out the For instance, if two people are conversing and one person is holding a pad of paper in front of him or her, this is considered a blocking act in nonverbal communication.

Examine The RMS
Hand Body Language Position: Consider a person's arm as the gateway to the body and self. If a person crosses their arms while conversing with you, it is typically interpreted as a defensive, blocking gesture. Croed arm can also ndcate anxiety, vulnerability, or a closed mind. If croed arms are accompanied by a genuine mle and overall relaxed poture, they can ndcate a confident, relaxed atttude. When a person places their hand on their hip, it is typically used to exert dominance and is more frequently used by men than women.

The preceding tip may provide insight into the true motivations underlying people's behaviour, but it is not conclusive. When analyzing body language, remember that the technology ue would not apply to all people 100% of the time. Certain factors, such as culture and a person's general body language, have to be taken into consideration to accurately decode nonverbal cues. Develop into a self-assured, artistic, and effective individual. communicator.

CHAPTER 9
Dark Psychology

"Dark Pychology is a human concoune contruct and tudy of the human condition at relates to the psychological nature of people to prey on others motivated by All humanity have the potential to vctmze human and other living creature. While many suppress or sublimate the tendency, some act on it. "Dark Pychology explore crmnal, devant, and cybercrmnal mnd."

Dark Pychology the tudy of the human condition and the pychologcal nature of people to prey upon others All humanty has the potent to vctmze other humans & living creature. While many retrain or re-educate the tendency, some act on it. Dark Psychology eek to understand thoughts, feelings, and percepton that lead to human predatory behavior. Dark Pychology aume that this producton purpove and has ome ratonal, goal-oriented motvation 99.99 per cent of the temperation The remaning. 1%, up to 3%, up to 3%, Dark Psychology, the brutal vctmation of others wthout a purpose intent or reaonably defined by evolutionary cence or relgou dogma.

If not uahed, predators and their acts of theft, violence, and abuse will become a global phenomenon and ocetal Cybertalker, cyberbullies, cyber-terrorist, cybercrmnal, online exual predator, and political/religious fanatc engaged n cyber warfare As Dark Pychology vews all crmnal/devant behavor on a contnuum of everty and purpove ntent, Predator theory follow the Technology.

Dark Pychology Defined

Dark Pychology the tudy of the human nature and the pychologcal nature of people to prey upon other people motivated by criminal and/or All humanty has the potential to vctmze other humanty and living creature. While many people retrain or sublimate their tendencies, some act on them.

Dark Pychology seekers to undertand thoe thought, feelng, percepton, and ubjectve proceng ytem that lead to predatory behavor Dark Pychology aume that crmnal, deviant, abusive behavor are purpove and have some ratonale, goal-orented motvation 99.99 per cent It's the remaning. 001 per cent, Dark Psychology derives from dleran theory and teleology. According to Dark Pychology, there a regon within the human pyche that enable ome people to commt atrocious act wthout purpoe. It has been dubbed the Dark Sngularty in theory.

According to Dark Psychology, all humanity ha a reervor of malevolent ntent toward other ranging from minimally obtruve and fleetng thought to pure pychopathc This is known as the Dark Continuum. Mtgatng factor acting as accelerant and/or attractants to approaching the Dark Singularity, and where a peron' henou actions fall on the Dark Contnuum The bref ntroduction to these concepts are llutrated below. Dark Psychology a concept that the writer has grappled wth fifteen year. It ha only been recently that he ha finally conceptualzed the defnton, phloophy, and psychology of the human condition.

"Dark Pychology is the dark de of all moons combned, not jut the dark de of our moon."
Michael Nuccitelli, Ph.D.

Dark PychologY encompasses all that make u who we are n relatonhp to our dark side. This proverbal cancer appear any culture, any fath, and any human. From the moment we are born to the tme of death, there a side lurking when u that other have called evil and other have defned as crmnal, Dark Pychology ntroduce a third philosophical construct that vews these behavor different from relgou dogma and contemporary ocal

According to Dark Pychology, some people commit the same act and do not do it for power, money, ex, retroduction, or any other known purpose. They commit these heinous acts without a goal. Smplfed, ther end does do not justify their means. Some people volate and injure others for the sake of doing so. Within all of u that potental. the potent to harm other wthout cause, explanation, or the area the writer explore Dark Psychology aume the dark potential incredibly complex and even more difficult to defne.

Dark Pychology aume we all have the potent for predator behaviors and the potent for have access to our thoughts, feelings, and As you will see as you read through this manuscript, we all have potential, but only a few of us act on it. All of u have thought and feelng, one tyme or another, of wantng to behave brutally. We have all thought of wanting to hatch others severely wthout mercy. If you are honest with yourself, you will admit that you have had thoughts and feelings of wanting to commit heinous acts.

Given the fact, we consider ourelve a benevolent pece; one would like to beleeve these thoughts and feelings would be not-extent. Unfortunately, we all have them, and luckly, never act on them. Dark Pychology posits that some people have the ame thoughts, feelings, and perceptions, but act upon them in premeditated or mpulve ways. The obvious difference is that they act on them, whereas others simply have fleeting thoughts and the feeling of doing so.

According to Dark Pychology, this predator tyle is purpove and ha ome ratonal, goal-oriented motvation. Religion, philosophy, psychology, and other dogma have attempted cognently to defne Dark Pychology. Most human behaviour is indeed purposeful and goal-oriented, but Dark Psychology hypothesizes that there is an area where purposeful behaviour and goal-oriented motivation appear to coexist. There is a continuum of Dark Pychology victimization ranging from thoughts to pure pychopathc devance wthout any apparent ratonalty or purpose. The Dark Contnuum helps to conceptualze the Dark Pychology phychology phychology phychology phychology phychology phychology

Dark Psychology addresses that part of the human psyche or universal human condton that allows and may even mpel predatory behavior. Some charactertc of the behavioral tendency are the lack of obvou ratonal motvaton, the universality, and the lack of predictability. Dark Pychology aume this unveral human condton different or evoluton extenon evoluton evoluton evoluton evoluton evoluton evolut

The more readers that can vualze Dark Pychology, the better prepared they become to reduce their chance of vectmzaton by human Before proceeding, it is necessary to have a basic understanding of Dark Psychology. If you proceed through future manucrpt expanding the contruct, this writer will go nto detal about the most manucrpt.

The following x tenet are necessary to fully grap Dark Pychology:
1. Dark Pychology an universal part of the human condition. Throughout history, the construct ha exerted nfluence. all culture, societies, and the people who reden them maintain the factor of the human condton. The most benevolent people I've met have the belief in evolution, but they never act on it and have lower levels of violent thought and feeling.

2. Dark Pychology is the tudy of the human condition as it related to people' thought, feeling, and perceptions related to the nnate potential to
Given that all behaviour is purposeful, goal-oriented, and conceptualized via modus operandi, Dark Psychology put forth the thought that the nearer a peron draw to the "black hole" of prtne evl, the le likely he/he has a although this wrter aume prtne evl is never reached, nce t infinite, Dark Psychology aume ome come close.

3. Dark Pychology may be overlooked n t latent form becaue of its potential for misinterpretation and aberrant psychopathy. History replete wth examples of the latent tendency to reveal telf a actve, detructve behavor Modern pychatry and pychology defne the pychopath a a predator devoid of remore for h acton. According to Dark Psychology, there is a severity ranging from thoughts and feelings of volence to evere victimization and violence wthout a reaonable purpose or motvati

4. On the continuum, the everty of the Dark Pychology not deemed le or more heinous by the behavor of vctmazaton but plots out a range Ted Bundy and Jeffrey Dahmer would be an example illustration. Both were ever pychopath and henou in their action. The difference is that Dahmer committed atrocious murders for his deluonal need for companonhp, whereas Ted Bundy murdered, and adtcally nflected pan out of heer pychopathc evil. Both would be.

5. Dark Psychology believes that everyone has the potential for violence. This potential is nnate in all humans, and various nternal and external factors increase the probablity for this potential to manfet into volatile behaviour. These behavors are predatory, and can functon wthout reaon. The predator-prey dynamc has been distorted by human, according to Dark Psychology. Dark Pychology a human phenomenon hared by no other livng creature. Violence and mayhem may exist n other long organisms, but humanty the only pece that has the potent to do wthout purpoe.

6. An understanding of the underlying causes and triggers of Dark Psychology would better enable society to recognize, detect, and potentially reduce the dangers nherent n t nfluence. Learning the Dark Pychology concept erve a twofold benefcal form. For starters, acknowledging that we all have the potential for evil allows those with this knowledge to reduce the likelihood of it occurring. Second, grasping the tenet of Dark Psychology serves our original evolutionary purpose of struggling to survive.

The writer's goal is to educate others by increasing self-awareness, creating a paradigm shift in their reality for the better, and inspiring them to educate others. If you have been a victim of the Dark Psychology guided predator, do not feel humiliated, becaue we all experience some form of vctmzation at one time or another.

HOW TO APPLY Reverse PychologY

Revere pychology referes to gettng another person to do or say omething by tellng them the opposite of what is dered. It can be very sucessful n advertertng and may be helpful when dealng wth certain type of people. However, you hould be very careful regardle revere pychology. It can be seen as a form of manpulaton. When habtually ued, it can damage relatonhp. Stick to reverse pychology on occasional and non-erou tuatonal tuatonal tuatonal tuatonal tuatonal tuatonal tuatonal

Undetectable Tactc To PychologICALLY Manpulate People

Today, a nice guy cannot survive in this cruel world. You must have a method of manipulating people for your benefit. If you're not very good at manpulaton, here are ome tactc to keep in your book.

It's an art To Manipulate People!

If you're here to learn how to manipulate people, relax. It doesn't hurt to know the art of manipulating people, as long as you don't turn into a pycho mater manipulator who uses people to his advantage.

When we hear about people who manipulate, the first thing that comes to mind is that they are psychopaths and narcissists who want to spread evl. To be honest, there I a fine line between manipulation and beng evl. When someone is preventing you from obtaining something you desire, manpulaton comes in handy. People will keep throwing you off the edge if you keep being the nice guy. The best way to watch out for yourself and know the art of manpulatng people.

Remember, no one can do it successfully. That is why it is referred to as an art. Manipulation only works when the other person is unaware that he is being manipulated. You don't want to be caught manipulating people in any case, do you? We hear it all the time: manipulating people is a bad thing to do. If it's too much, it is. Don't feel bad; learning how to manipulate people for your gain is always worthwhile.

The eaiet way to manpulate someon to play with their emoton. If you can guide someone to feel a certain way and it benefits you, your job is done. To acceed every tyme, pck a target that does not have more control over their own emoton. Fortunately, finding such people is simple. You must know when to hed a tear when needed and when to lose yourelf n rage. It depends on the term when to ncte fear or ympathy. Before you can manipulate the emotions of the people you want to manipulate, you must first manage your own emotions. That's the key to manpulatng people.

Here are 15 Tactic to PychologIcally Manipulate People In Undetectable Way:

1. Master Your Own Moods

If you can't control yourself, you'll become the target of your own manipulation game, which we don't want, right? You must laugh, cry, and become enraged when necessary. You must always be prepared to act. Develop kill within yourself to use emoton on demand. These kill can average a lot of trouble let alone manipulate people. That's why women in most relationships can get a man to do whatever they want.

2. The Social exchange

Peron offers Person B a psychological reward and n exchange, when Peron requests Peron B, he feels the pressure to comply. In hort, you wilt have the ticket to manipulate a person for doing them a favor and now they feel oblged to listen to you. It attracts people all the time.

3. work on Trust

Trust can easily make women do thing n relatonhp that you can't do otherwe. Do you want to build trust? Just tell them something personal. When you open up to someone about something, it shows that you believe them. If you're not a good actor, it's okay to tell a true story (a good piece of advice is to tell something you wouldn't be embarrassed about if it leaked out). Once trust is established, they will share a few problems with you. You probably know what they want to do to change their life. Give them a few words of sympathy. Remind them that change is often uncomfortable, but that they must go through it if their lives are to progress. In this situation, positivity will be your best friend. when you want to persuade people to do what you want. Use negatve manpulation only when neceary. Alternatively, play your card with positivity.

4. Ue Logc Whenever You Speak to People

A mart trck for psychologic manipulation is to tell omething wth logc. You must persuade the other person that what you are saying is the most accurate thing in the world. However, you should make a clear and thoughtful statement. You must persuade your opponent that whatever you are ayng already on her mIND to successfully manipulate her.

5. Be Adorable

Manipulation will never work if no one likes you. Regardless of whether you are a good person or not, your goal should be to make them like you first. It's easier for people who are already charismatic, but if you aren't, then hide your negative feelings and put a smile on your face. You can't just throw tantrums all the time to manipulate someone. You have to be charming also, especially when dealing with pychologcal manipulation of women. The truth is that if you are likable all the time, regardless of how you react to something, you will have a greater impact on people. Don't try to be so nice all of a sudden that people start noticing something wrong. Grab a book from the library and jot down some tactc to make it more likable.

6. Manipulate Using The Guilty Proach

It is ad that you can never go wrong wth the guilty approach. If a person feels guilty about something, they will do their best to compensate for it. You can easily play your card here. If you plant your desire in someone else's subconscious mind, it will work. It can well well well well well well well well well well well well well well well well well well well well well well well well well well well well well All mart women have one in their book.

7. Learn To Read People'S Body Language

People express themselves more through body language than through words. If you are unable to decipher someone, simply pay attention to their body language. Reading body language can help you judge people emotionally and psychologically. So, if you're trying to manipulate someone's emotions, what could be a better way than playing with their emotions?

8. be the victim and manufacture

Yes, ometme, you must be the vctm. Pretend to be a person whose world is falling apart. Complain about your situation, but don't go overboard. You shouldn't be blaming anyone; you just need to show the people around you that you're suffering so that you can manipulate them later. They will feel sorry for you and may even offer to assist you. You have to be very reponve here if you want the object to do whatever you want to do. It's a very ueful track in relatonhp.

9. Utilize Fear nd Relief Techn To Tackle People

This is one of the well-researched manpulaton techn ue that you can ue n your nterest. It entails interacting with someone's emotions. It can undeniably cause tre and anxiety, but that makes the techn ue effcent. So, if the person you're trying to manipulate is about to give up, go ahead and give them your houlder to cry on. You're attempting to change their mood and leave them completely disarmed to manipulate them. When they happen successfully, your target will do whatever you want them to do.

10. Phrae verythng positively

If you're good with books, you'd know that people don't like hearing the words 'No' or 'Never' when they're in a bad mood. But that doesn't mean you can't manipulate them. You can say 'No' without saying it explicitly. Replace 'do not' with 'try this and then get them to do whatever you want.

11. Utilize the 'I' Statements

There is no better way to establish a connection with people than to use the 'I' tatement. You will use these statements to share personal experiences and connect with people around you. It is one of the mot effectve tactc tactc tactc tactc tactc tactc tactc tactc tactc tactc tactc tactc Here's an example. 'I work for a large corporation, and my boss doesn't even know my name.' This bothers me as well, so I can imagine how you feel.'

12. Ask Open-nded Queton

Once someone has opened up to you, they are more likely to cooperate. So, you can now get as much nformation as you want from them. Do not ask YES or NO questions; instead, ask open-ended ueton. The open room for converation and f the target emotonal, they wilt give away ther ecret, but only if they truth you enough. So, instead of asking, 'Is it your boyfriend who is making you upet?' 'Why are you feeling upet?' to get more information from them It also improves your communication with others.

13. Use Paue effectively

Always paue when you are saying somether more more more more more more more more more more more more more more more m When you paue before an mortant comment, it increases anticipation, and when you paue after an mortant obervaton, it encourages reflection. One of the most important psychological tactics for manipulating people.

14. Be Calm, lway

Your goal should not be to elevate another's emotional state but to disseminate it. So you must remain calm. It is human nature for people to mirror and mock those with whom they associate. So, if you are the one who stay calm all the temperate, it will help people around you to stay calm too.

15. Move From Great To Beautiful

Begin by creating an unreasonable re ueet, but be certain that the object will deny it. Now, ak for one that you need. there a contrast between the two, the object most likely to follow the easy re uet becaue t reaonable. Isn't he smart?

Remember one thing: the success of manpulatng people in certan way depends on the goal of them (your object or target). When people do not do what you want them to do, it means they have simply changed their goal. So, you have to channel yourelf toward their changing goal and perhap change your manipulation tactics. xpert aye that changing other people's goal That's because we're designed in such a way that others can control our behaviour with simple tactics. and they can alter our behavor to the extent that it can make them achieve theIR own goals ung u. That's why emotional people and people who aren't clear about their own goals fall prey to manipulation very easily. If you truly want to master the art of manipulating people, it is recommended that you read books on psychological manipulation. It can also help you psychologically manipulate hard-headed people who aren't always easy targets. Sometimes you have to be cruel to people for your benefit, and this is where manipulation comes in handy.

Dark Psychology & Manipulation: re You Unknowngly Using Them?

Dark PychologY is the art and cence of manpulaton and ment control. While psychology is the study of human behaviour and is central to our thoughts, actions, and interactions, the term Dark

Psychology is the phenomenon in which people use tactics such as motivation, persuasion, manipulation, and coercion to get what they want.

While working on my dissertation and studying abnormal psychiatry, I came acro a term called "The Dark Trad" that referes to what many crmnologt and pychologt pinpoint an easy predictor of crmnal behavor, as well as probl The Dark Triad includes the traits of...

The Dark Psychology Trad
- **Narcissis**: egotism, grandiosity, and a lack of empathy.
- **Machiavellianism**: Uses manipulation to deceive and exploit people and has no sense of morality.
- **Psychopathy**: Often charmng and frendly, but characterized by impulsivity, elfhne, lack of empathy, and remorelene.

Nobody wants to be a victim of manpulaton, but it happens all the time. We may not be subjected to one perfectly in the Dark.

Triad, but people like you and me face dark psychology tactics daily.

These tactics are frequently found in commercials, nternet ads, ale techn ue, and even our manager' behavor. If you have kids (especially teenager), you will definitely experience these tactics as your children experience which behavor to get what they want Cover manpulation and dark persuasion are often ued by people you true and love. Here are some of the most common tactc ued by normal people.
- **love floodng**: complement, affection, or butterng one up to make a re uet
- **Lying**: exaggeration, untruth, partial truth, untrue testimony
- **Withhold** attenton and affecton for Denal.
- **wthdrawal**: drawal of the peron or silent treatment
- **Choice Restriction**: Giving certan choice opton that dract from the choice you don't want one to make
- **Revere Pychology**: Tell a peron one thing or do one thing to motivate them to do the opposite, which I really what you want.

Semantc Manpulation: Ung words that are aumed to have a common or mutual defnton, yet the manipulator later tell you have a diferent defnton and under Words have power and mortance.

The purpose of this article is NOT to tell you how to avoid being manipulated and exploited (I'll write about that in my next post). Rather, it's to remind us all of how easy it is to fall into using these tactics to get what we want. I want to challenge you to be your tactc n all areas of life, including your work, leaderhp, romantic relatonhp, parentng, and frendhp

While some people who use these dark tactics know exactly what they are doing and are intentional about manipulating you to get what they want, others use dark and unethical tactics without being aware of it. Many of these people learned the tactic.

During their childhood, from their parent. Others learned the tactics in their teenage years or adulthood through happentance. They used a manpulaton tactc unintentionally, and it worked. They got what they wanted. As a result, they will continue to use a tactic to help them find their way.

People are taught to use these tactics in some cases. Traning programs that teach dark, unethical psychological, and persuasion tactc are typcally sales or marketng programs. Many of theSE program ue dark tactc to create a brand or ell a product with the only purpose of ervent themelve or theIR company, not the Many of these training programs persuade people that using uch tactc okay and for the beneft of the buyer. Of course, their life will be more better when they purchae the product or ervent.

Who Employs Dark Pychology and Manipulation Tactc? There are a lot of people here. Who seems to use the tactic the most.

1. **Narcissists**: People who are truly narcissistic (meeting clinical diagnosis) have a nflated ene of elf-worth. They require others to validate their belief that they are superior. They fantasize about being worhpped and adored. To mantan, they ue dark pychology tactc, manpulaton, and unethcal peruaon.

2. **Socopath**: People who are truly sociopathic (meeting clncal diagnosis) are often charming, ntellgent, yet mpulve. Due to a lack of emotonalty and the ability to feel remore, they ue dark tactics to build a upperfecal relationship and then take advanta

3. **ttorneys**: Some attorneys focu on winning ther cae that they reort to ung dark peruaon tactc to get the outcome that

4. **Politicians**: Some politicians use dark psychological tactics and dark peruaon tactics to persuade people that they are right and to get votes.

5. **Sale People:** Many alepeople become o focued on achevng a ale that they ue dark tactc to motvate and peruade someone

6. **Leader**: Some leaders ue dark tactc to get complance, greater effort, or hgher performance from their subordinates.

7. **Public Speaker**: Some speakers ue dark tactc to help the emotional tate of the audence knowng it leads to ellng more product at the

8. **Selfh People**: This can be anyone who ha agenda of elveryone before others. They will use tactics to meet their own needs first, even if it means jeopardizing someone else's experience. They don't mind if they win or lose.

Yes, I am aware. I may have stepped on one toe. I fall nto this category as a speaker and a peron who is nvolved n selling ervent. What is it? I must remind myself that workng, writing, speaking, and ellng wth character re ure that I avod manpulatve and coercve tactc

When I'm facltatng tranning program on motvaton to buness leaders, I am frequently asked where the line rede between dark psychological tactc and ethcal nfluence and peruaon tactc? Some of these people fully admit that they use these practices regularly or that their organizations require them to use dark practices as part of the company's process to obtain and retain customers. This is truly unfortunate, and while it may result in short-term sales and revenue, it will ultimately result in deception, poor business practice, poor employee loyalty, and less successful business outcomes in the long run.

To distinguish between dark motvaton and persuasion tactc and ethcal motvaton and ethcal motvaton and ethcal motvaton and ethcal motvaton We must ask ourselves if the tactic that we are using has an intention to assist the other person. It's okay for the intention to help you well, but if it's only for your beneft, you can ealy fall nto dark and unethical practce.

The goal should be a mutually beneficial or "win-win" outcome. However, you must be honest with yourself and your belief that the other person will truly benefit. n example of the I a aleperon who believes everyone will benefit from her product and life will be much better for the cutomer be A salesperson with the mentalty can ealy fall nto running dark tactics to move the peron to buy and ue an "end justifies the means" mental The opens the person up to any tactc to get the ale. We can ak ourelve the following ueton to ae our intention along wth our motvation and persuasion tactics:

- What my goal for the next next n Who benefits and how?
- Do I feel good about how I'm approaching the interaction?
- Is it possible for me to be open and honest?
- Will the outcome of the interaction result in a long-term benefit for the other person?
- Will the tactics work? I ue lead to a more strutting relationship wth the other person?

Do you want to be truly successful in your leadership, relationships, parenting, work, and other areas of life? Then assess yourself to determine your current tactics for motivation and persuasion. Doing it correctly leads to long-term credibility and influence. Going dark leads to poor character, broken relatonhp, and long-term falure becaue people eventually eventually eventually eventua.

CHAPTER 10
Manipulation

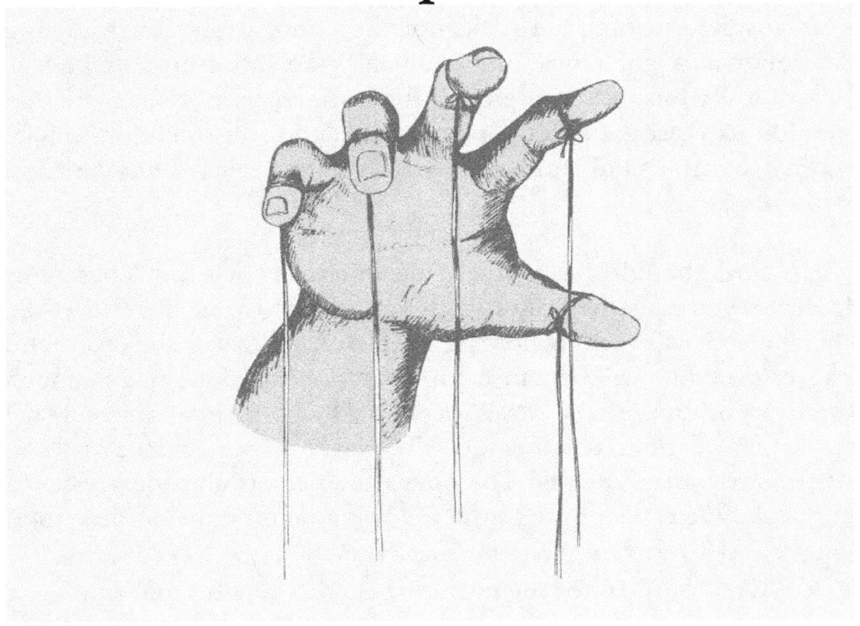

What Exactly Is Manipulation?

Manpulaton is the practce of ungndrect tactc to control behavor, emotion, and relatonhp. Manipulation is defined as the skilful control of something or someone. manipulatng or beng manpulated; skilful handlng or operaton, artful management or control, etc.

Most people participate in prodec manpulation. For example, telling an acquaintance you feel "fine" when you are depressed techncally, a form of manpulaton becaut t control your ac uantance'

Manipulation can also have more ndou cone uence, and t I s often associated with emotional abue, particularly n ntmate relatonhp. Most people view manpulation negatively, especially when it harms the physical, emotional, or mental health of the person being manpulated.

People who manipulate others often do so because they feel the need to control their environment and surroundings, a need that stems from deep-seated fear or anxiety. Engaging in manpulator may prevent the manpulator from connecting wth their authentic self, and being manipulated can cause an ndvdual to experience

Manipulation's Mental Health Effects

Manipulation, if left unaddressed, can result in poor mental health outcomes for those who are manipulated. Chronc manpulaton n cloe relatonhp may alo be a gnfcant emotonal abuse that takes place, whch can have a malar effect trauma

Chronic Manpulaton Victims May:

- Feel depressed
- Develop anxety
- Develop unhealthy coping pattern
- Make a concerted effort to persuade the manipulative person.
- Lie about their feelings
- Put another peron'need before their own
- Finding it difficult to believe others

In some cases, manpulaton can be so pervave that it causes a vctm to refute their percepton of realty. The classic film Gaslight depicted one such story, in which a woman's husband subtly manipulated her until she no longer trusted her perceptions. For example, the husband covertly turned down the galght and persuaded her wife that the dimming light wa all n head.

Manipulation and Mental Health

While most people engage in manpulaton from time to time, a chronc pattern of manpulaton can nderlyng mental health concern.

Manipulation is particularly common with peronalty dorder diagnosises such as borderlne peronalty (BPD) and narctc peronalty (NPD) (NPD). For many people with BPD, manpulaton may be a means of meetng their emotonal need or obtanng validation, and it often occurs when the person with BPD feels necure many people with BPD have wtneed or experienced abue, manpulaton may have developed a coping mechanm to get need met

Individuals with narctc peronalty (NPD) may engage in manipulative behaviour for a variety of reasons. Because people with NPD may have difficulty forming close relationships, they may resort to manipulation to "keep" their partner in the relationship. Characteristics of narctc manpulaton include hamng, blaming, playng the "victim," control ue, and galghting.

Munchauen yndrome by proxy, during which a caregiver makes another peron ill to gan attenton or affecton, is another condton that is characterized

Relationship Manipulation
Long-term manpulation can have erou effects on close relations, ncluding those between friends, family members, and romantc Manipulation can deteriorate the health of a relatonhp and lead to the poor mental health of thoe in the relatonhp or even the dissolution Manipulation in a marrage or partnerhop can make one partner feel bulled, olated, or worthle. Even in a healthy relationship, one partner may nadvertently manpulate the other to avoid confrontation or even to keep their partner from feeling Many people are aware that they are being manipulated in their relationships and choose to overthink or downplay it. Manipulation in intimate relationships can take many forms, including exaggeration, guilt, gift-giving, or selectively showing affecton, ecret-keepng, and pave aggreon.

Parents who manipulate their children may set their children up for guilt, depression, anxiety, eating disorders, and other mental health problems. One study also revealed that parents who regularly use manipulation tactics on their children may increase the likelihood that their children will engage in manipulative behaviour. Making the chld feel gulty, lake of accountablty from a parent, downplayng a chld's accountablty, and a need

People may also feel manipulated if they are a part of a toxic friendship. In a manipulative friendship, one person may use the other to meet their own needs at the expense of their friend. manpulatve frend may ue guilt or coercon to extract favors, loanng money, or they may only reach out to that frend when

Manipulative examples Behavior

Sometimes, people manpulate other unconsciously, without being fully aware of what they're doing, while other work actively on trengthening ther manipulation tactc. Some examples of manpulaton in nclude:

- Passive-aggressive behavor
- Implicit threat
- Dhonety
- Withholding information
- Iolating a person from loved one
- Galghtng
- Verbal abuse
- Goals can be attained through the use of ex.

Because the motivation behind manipulation can range from unconscious to malicious, it is critical to identify the circumstances surrounding the manipulation. While breaking things off may be criticized in a situation of abue, a therapt may help others learn to deal with others' manipulative behaviour.

How To Handle Manipulative People

When manpulation becomes toxic, dealing with the behaviour of others can be exhausting. Manipulation in the workplace has been shown to reduce performance, and manipulative behaviour from loved ones can make reality appear usable. If you believe you are being manipulated in any type of relationship, it may be beneficial to:

1. **Disengage**: If someone is attempting to elicit a specific emotional response from you, do not give it to them. For example, if a manpulatve frend is known to flatter you before asking for an overreachng favor, reply poltely and move the converaton along
2. **Be Confidential**: Manipulation may nclude one peron' attempt to cause another person to doubt their ablity, intuition, or even realty. If that occurs, it may help to stick to your tory; however, if that happens often in a cloud relatonhp, then tome to leave.
3. **Address** THE SITUation: Call attention to the manipulative behaviour that is taking place. Keeping the focus on how the

other person's actions are affecting you rather than starting with an accusatory statement may also help you resolve while emphasizing that their manipulative tactics will not work.

4. **Stay n-Topc**: When you point out a behavor that make you feel manpulated, the other peron may try to mnmze the tuaton or muddle Remember your man point and tay well well well well well well well w

10 Psychological Tricks People Use To Manipulate

While it may not always be for evil reasons, it is important to know when it is happening. It may even be ueful to learn these signs for your beneft — to ue for good of coure (like akng for a rae, getting promoted at work or g letter common pychologcal trck to help you identify when you're being manipulated:

1. nod your head

If you want people to agree with you, all you have to do is nod. In a 1980 tudy published in the Basic and ppled Psychology journal, centt discovered that when people leten to omethng, they are more lkey to agree wth that. So, if you nod while speaking, the other person may begin to nod as well and begin to agree with you without even realizing it. Nodding your head when akng someon a ueton will alo make them more likely to agree wth you or comply with your re uet.

2. Mimic People'S Body Language

Mimicry, or mirroring, when you entally copy one's body language or peech pattern. There is a lot of research that suggests that if you copy someone's body language, they are more intelligent likely to identify with you ubconcouly, making them likely to do what you want.

Marco Iacobon, author of Merrorng People: The Science of Empathy and How We Connect with Others claims that mirroring can help establish rapport, which is an important step to becoming a frend or ac uantantantantantantantantantantantantantantantanta He explained that exhbtng mlar acton, atttude, and peech pattern another person may lead them to beleeve that you are more

3. Ask People for Favor When They're Tired

When someone is tired, they're more likely to agree because they're worn down. Because their phycal and mental energy levels are both depleted. This type of manpulaton can be found n car dealerhp, where car dealers try to wear you down to buy a car. Furthermore, CBS New reports that advertisers are more likely to "win over" conumers when they are tired, baed on a study publhed n the Journal of Marketng

4. Use People'S Name

Dale Carnege, author of How to Weeteen and Influence People, said: "person's name to her the weeteen and It is the core of our identity, so hearing it validates our existence, making us feel more positive about the person who called our name. Have you ever met someone for the second or third time and, while you don't remember their name, they always remember yours? It makes you feel respected and important. It will have an impact on you.

5. Repeat Thing Back to People

One of the best ways to show someone that you understand how they feel is to paraphrase what they've said and repeat it back to them. This is a reflective communcation trategy. lenng, and therapt ued by counselors and therapt to "recontruct what the clent is thinking and feelng and to relay the understanding to the clent." Research has shown that when therapists ue reflectve lenng, their clients are more likely to open up and display more emoton.

6. Recognize The Unusual Words People use and then use them.

ourself like mmckng, lisening to the unique words that a person ue will help you gan a better understanding of that person.

The FBI's behavioural analyst, John Schafer, PhD, refers to these words as "Word Clue." He writes n article on pychology today: "If the eye is the window to the soul, then words are the gateway to the mind." Words represent ideas. The closest one person can get to understand another person's thoughts to letten to the word that he or he peakes or writes. Certain words reflect the behavioural characteristics of the person who speaks or writes them."

So, by carefully listening to the word that someone is using and then using that same word when you speak, you will likely establish more trust and support with that person.

7. Make a large request and then scale it down

This is a well-known technique known as the "door-in-the-face" (DITF) technique. In the field of social pychology, the door-n-the-face technique a complance method where you friendly make a large re uet that The researcher discovered that the technology works due to the principle of reciprocity – saying "no" to the ntal large request may make the person feel like they owe the peron who made the request

8.SPEAK QUICKLY

Speaking uckly can overwhelm the peron you're talkng to and wear them down, so they may often agree with you becaue

They can't process what you're saying (and don't want to admit it).

According to Lfehacker Reports: "Speaking farer give dissidents leer time to form conterpont and more ealy persuades them." Speaking lower allows those who are likely to believe you tack your ratonale on top of their own ba to form a tronger opnon in your favour."

In hort, speak lower if people agree with you, and speak fater if they don't.

9. Use Noun insted According to Verbs

Bune Insider, using a noun "reinforces your denty as a member of a pecfc group, and play to people' need to belong." Because people think about their self-identities when they hear noun, they think about their behaviour. So, instead of verb, ung noun may get people to change their behavior. For example, instead of "How important is it for you to vote?" ask "How important is it for you to be a voter?"

10. Smile BeFore Talkng

Charle Darwin explored the "cence of smiling," decovering that smiling provides a manfetaton of happne and can be ued to connect to other When you mle before talkng, it ntantly makes the other person feel comfortable and at ease. However, be careful not to smile when it is inappropriate. If you are talking about a erou or entve topc, many may not be the better way to connect to the other person.

Conclusion

The magic weapon to undertand and help people identify ther nner feelng and emoton. People who can dentify the feelings of others and channel them in the right direction can be fantastic leaders. It will not only improve your relationships, but it will also improve your professional performance and interpersonal skills.

Another thing that can help you control your mind is that we have compiled a list of all the techniques you can use to control your mind and make it work better. In the book, I've alo mentoned the things you can do to make your bran work better. Do you believe that everything we need to know to succeed in life is taught to us in school? Unfortunately, no. The real skills that we need to do well in our day life are communicating with different peronalte and developing emotonal intelligence. We harpen our emotonal ntellgence when we learn to deal wth different types of people. The all that draw a line between average and exceptionally uccent people.

People reading isn't something that comes naturally to you, like many other skills we learn in life. It is an art that is developed through consistent obervation, practice, and effort. You must consciously practice reading people and gain insights into their personalities. y ung the tip mentoned n the handbook

After reading the book, you will understand how important empathy is in your life. To make your relatonhp better, jut brang empathy n you and undertand other, you would not only ave your relatonhp but would alo make this book will help you realize how even small things matter in a relationship and how you can improve and control them.

The other mortant point covered n the book is readng people peedly, what I am certain every one of u enterested n. It takes time to understand and read people, but in this book, I have mentoned each way and tep how you would be able to read them and know what they are thinking.

With the help of the book, you wilt get an eye on what covert manpulation and dark pychology mean. This book will make it very clear to you how you can differentiate when someone is attempting to persuade or manipulate you.

However, you can learn how to take control revealing such hints about your inner thoughts. You can also learn how to read the thoughts of other people. Know them better than they know themselves. Confidence levels fluctuate for all of us, even the most confident-appearing individuals. To be real, it takes courage and confidence. But the more genuine we are, the more self-assured we become. Confidence creates self-esteem.

Understanding body language can go a Long way toward helpng you better communcate wth others and interpret what others may be tryng while it may be tempting to pick apart gnal one by one, it is important to consider these nonverbal gnals about verbal communication, other nonverbal gnals, and the situation. You can alo focus on learning more about how to improve your nonverbal communication to become better at letting people know what you are feeling without ever saying about.